THE JOURNAL OF ARCHITECTURE, DESIGN & DOMESTIC SPACE

VOLUME TWO
ISSUE THREE
NOVEMBER 2005

HOME
CULTURES

SPECIAL ISSUE: THE DOMESTIC
INTERIOR IN BRITISH LITERATURE

BERG

AIMS AND SCOPES

Home Cultures is an interdisciplinary journal dedicated to the critical understanding of the domestic sphere, its artefacts, spaces and relations, across timeframes and cultures. Whether as a concept or a physical place, "home" is a highly fluid and contested site of human existence that reflects and reifies identities and values. The Journal aims to promote a conversation about the domestic sphere across the many disciplines in which 'home' forms a key unit of analysis. By generating a site for interdisciplinary discussion and comparative approaches, *Home Cultures* provides a vital and diverse forum for our general understanding of this vital sphere of human activity.

Towards this aim, the editors invite submissions from a broad range of scholars and practitioners, including: design practices, design history, social history, literary studies, architecture, gender studies, cultural/social history, anthropology, sociology, archaeology, urban planning, legal studies, contemporary art, geography, psychology, folklore, cultural studies, literary studies and art history.

Home Cultures is indexed by HW Wilson and IBSS (International Bibliography of Social Sciences)

Typeset by JS Typesetting Ltd, Porthcawl, Mid Glamorgan
Printed in the UK

Anyone wishing to submit an article, interview, book, film or exhibition review for possible publication in this journal should contact the editors at,

homecultures@ucl.ac.uk

Notes for contributors can be found at the back of the journal.

©2005 Berg. All rights reserved. No part of this publication may be reproduced or utilized in any form or by any means, electronic or mechanical, including photocopying and recording, or by any information storage or retrieval system, without permission in writing from the publisher.

ISSN: 1740-6315

SUBSCRIPTION INFORMATION

Three issues per volume.
One volume per annum.
2005: Volume 2

ONLINE
www.bergpublishers.com

BY MAIL
Berg Publishers
C/o Customer Services
Extenza-Turpin
Pegasus Drive
Stratton Business Park
Biggleswade
Bedfordshire SG18 8TQ
UK

BY FAX
+44 (0)1767 601640

BY TELEPHONE
+44 (0)1767 604800

INQUIRIES
Editorial: Kathryn Earle, Managing Editor, email: kearle@bergpublishers.com
Production: Ken Bruce, email: kbruce@bergpublishers.com
Advertising and subscriptions: Veruschka Selbach, email: vselbach@bergpublishers.com

SUBSCRIPTION RATES
Institutions' subscription rate £130/US$225
Individuals' subscription rate £45/US$78*

*This price is available only to personal subscribers and must be prepaid by personal cheque or credit card

Free online subscription for print subscribers

Full color images available online

Access your electronic subscription through www.ingenta.com or www.ingentaselect.com

REPRINTS FOR MAILING
Copies of individual articles may be obtained from the publishers at the appropriate fees.
Write to

Berg Publishers
1st Floor, Angel Court
81 St Clements Street
Oxford OX4 1AW
UK

EDITORS

Victor Buchli
University College London, UK

Alison Clarke
University of Applied Arts, Vienna, Austria

Dell Upton
University of Virginia, USA

ADVISORY BOARD

Judith Attfield, Winchester School of Art, University of Southampton, UK

Leora Auslander, University of Chicago, USA

Iain Borden, The Bartlett School of Architecture, University College London, UK

Peter Burke, University of Cambridge, UK

Sophie Chevalier, Université de Franche-Comté, France

Irene Cieraad, Delft University of Technology, Netherlands

Elizabeth Cromley, Northeastern University, USA

Inge Daniels, AHRB Centre for the Study of the Domestic Interior, UK

Prof. Sir Christopher Frayling, Rector of the Royal College of Art, UK

Alice Friedman, Wellesley College, USA

Paul Groth, University of California at Berkeley, USA

Craig Gurney, Cardiff University, UK

Ian Hodder, Stanford University, USA

Miwon Kwon, University of California at Los Angeles, USA

Orvar Löfgren, University of Lund, Sweden

Ellen Lupton, Maryland Institute College of Art, USA

Lydia Martens, University of Durham, UK

Kathy Mezei, Simon Fraser University, Canada

Daniel Miller, University College London, UK

Gerald Pocius, Memorial University of Newfoundland, Canada

Martin Raymond, Viewpoint, UK

Suzanne Reimer, University of Southampton, UK

Elizabeth Shove, University of Lancaster, UK

Ilya Utekhin, European University at St Petersburg, Russia

US EXHIBITION REVIEWS
Shelley Nickles, Smithsonian National Museum of American History, USA

UK BOOK & EXHIBITION REVIEWS
Clare Melhuish, Buckinghamshire Chilterns University College, UK

HOME CULTURES
VOLUME TWO
ISSUE THREE
NOVEMBER 2005

CONTENTS

229 Guest Editorial
CHARLOTTE GRANT

233 Reading the House of Fiction: From Object to Interior 1720–1920
CHARLOTTE GRANT

251 Modernism, the City and the "Domestic Interior"
MORAG SHIACH

269 Early Modern Plays and Domestic Spaces CATHERINE RICHARDSON

285 Evidence, Experience and Conjecture: Reading the Interior through Benjamin and Bloch CHARLES RICE

299 Reproducing the Home in Robert Tressell's *The Ragged Trousered Philanthropists* and D. H. Lawrence's *Sons and Lovers* NICOLA WILSON

GUEST EDITORIAL
CHARLOTTE GRANT

AHRC CENTRE FOR THE STUDY
OF THE DOMESTIC INTERIOR

> This *Home Cultures* special issue looks at the representation of the home, specifically the domestic interior, in literature in Britain. Articles from a range of methodological perspectives focus on particular historical moments from the early modern to modernism. The authors came together as participants at a conference on literature and the domestic interior organized as part of the work of the AHRC Centre for the Study of the Domestic Interior. Based in London at the Royal College of Art, CSDI is an AHRC funded research centre run in collaboration with the Victoria and Albert Museum, and Royal Holloway, University of London. The Centre's core project is an examination of the representation of domestic interiors in text and image from the Renaissance to the present, identifying moments of change and shared modes of representation from the renaissance to the contemporary. In the course of CSDI's conference on literature and the domestic interior, the particular moments discussed here emerged as important points of reference in that changing narrative.

In the first article, I look at the etymological history that links the "interior" to the mental "inward" and connect both to the development of fiction. This is a broadly historical account from Defoe through Dickens to Woolf which differentiates between literary representations of the domestic interior in terms of varying narrative styles. Morag Shiach picks up the question of the place of the domestic interior in literary modernism, arguing that the focus on spectacle and the modern city in the critical focus on the "*flâneur*" and latterly "street haunting," have led to a marginalization of the domestic interior. She also challenges the assumption that the interior is equated with the familial-domestic, unsettling gendered assumptions in her readings of Woolf, Richardson and Pound.

The three following authors concentrate on different historical moments. Catherine Richardson's discussion of pre-Restoration theatre practice analyzes the role of the imagination in the representation of the interior through a discussion of the mechanics of staging in the early modern period. Her comparative analysis of the domestic interior in city comedies and domestic tragedies draws a contrast between the representation of the social and the personal, a theme which emerges as a preoccupation of later periods. Charles Rice discusses the domestic interior in relation to the nineteenth-century detective story. He brings together Carlo Ginzburg's understanding of the story as a "conjectural" form of knowledge with both the process of murder detection (as in Sherlock Holmes), and Freud's notion of the uncanny, as well as Benjamin on the historical emergence and collapse of the bourgeois interior, and Ernst Bloch on detective fiction. Finally, Nicola Wilson's article reads the domestic interior in relation to class, concentrating on two key texts for twentieth-century working-class writing in Britain. Her reading of Robert Tressell's *The Ragged Trousered Philanthropists* illuminates complex arguments about family, class, the form of wages and household management, and her analysis of D.H. Lawrence's *Sons and Lovers* evokes the domestic interior in terms of its psychic dangers for smotherable men.

Together these articles give an insight into current approaches to the analysis of the literary representation of the domestic interior. They represent an area of study, which, in common with other approaches to the home, especially those from material culture studies, is transforming the way we look at the home, its history, and the histories and modes of its representation across a wide range of media.

CHARLOTTE GRANT
READING THE HOUSE OF FICTION: FROM OBJECT TO INTERIOR 1720–1920

CHARLOTTE GRANT IS SENIOR RESEARCH FELLOW AT THE AHRC CENTRE FOR THE STUDY OF THE DOMESTIC INTERIOR, A COLLABORATION BETWEEN THE ROYAL COLLEGE OF ART, THE VICTORIA AND ALBERT MUSEUM AND THE BEDFORD CENTRE, ROYAL HOLLOWAY, UNIVERSITY OF LONDON. SHE HAS PUBLISHED ON EIGHTEENTH-CENTURY LITERATURE AND VISUAL AND MATERIAL CULTURE, AND IS CO-EDITOR, WITH JEREMY AYNSLEY, OF *IMAGINED INTERIORS: REPRESENTING THE DOMESTIC INTERIOR SINCE THE RENAISSANCE* (V&A PUBLICATIONS, 2006).

This article traces a line through the representation of the domestic interior in British fiction from the 1720s to the 1920s. It argues that during this period the emphasis of description shifts from the enumeration of objects surrounding fiction's protagonists towards invoking a sense of the domestic interior itself, and that this move can be linked to the novel's varying relationship to, and questioning of, narrative realism. Starting from Henry James's phrase "the house of fiction," it asks whether his metaphor and the related association between the interior and interiority are anything more than linguistic fortuity. Focusing on the narrative modes described as "free indirect discourse" and "stream of consciousness," it argues that authors exploit the flexibility of narrative styles to represent both the domestic interior, and the consciousness or interiority of its inhabitants, and that even when challenged, this association is key to understanding fiction's representation of the home in this period.

> There were two other rooms, beyond the one in which she had been received, equally full of romantic objects, and in these apartments Isabel spent a quarter of an hour. Everything was in the last degree curious and precious, and Mr Osmond continued to be the kindest of ciceroni as he led her from one fine piece to another and still held his little girl by the hand. His kindness almost surprised our young friend, who wondered why he should take so much trouble for her; and she was oppressed at last with the accumulation of beauty and knowledge to which she found herself introduced. (James 1995: 287)

Descriptions of houses, their interiors, and the objects found in them, feature with varying degrees of detail from the early prose fiction of the eighteenth century through to contemporary novels. Clearly different depictions are used to different rhetorical effect, and their function depends on the many particular circumstances of each individual novel, author, and reader. It is perhaps in the nineteenth century that such depictions are most prevalent, as in the heroine's first visit to her future husband's house in Henry James's *The Portrait of a Lady* (1881) quoted above. The novel opens with afternoon tea in an English country garden and moves through a series of English houses to Italy and back. The "portrait" is of Isabel Archer, the American heroine, and the novel charts her struggle against the man she marries, Gilbert Osmond, the "cicerone" of the quotation above, who attempts to constrain her three-dimensional life, rendering her an ornament in his collection of "romantic objects." In this novel the narrative turns on the heroine's refusal to conform to the status of property: Isabel Archer cannot be reduced to an artifact in an inventory, a "portrait of a lady"; her sense of destiny transcends her material circumstances. The novel is, in common with others by Henry James, such as *The Wings of a Dove* (1902), intimately concerned with property, and with the place of the domestic interior as a place of dreams and aspirations, and their realization or thwarting.

In his 1909 preface to the New York edition of *The Portrait of a Lady*, James develops an extended metaphor describing the current state of "the house of fiction." In James's image authors look out onto the outside world through the windows of a house:

> The spreading field, the human scene, is the "choice of subject," the pierced aperture, wither broad or balconied or slit-like and

low-browed, is the "literary form" but they are, singly, or together, as nothing without the presence of the watcher—without, in other words, the consciousness of the artist. (James 1995: 8)

Each author sees differently according to their place in the house, the viewpoint their window gives them, and their own experience. Fiction then does not merely depict houses and their interiors, it is, for James, itself a house. A similar metaphor fuels "The Novel Démeublé," an essay by Willa Cather, who complains about the level of detail in nineteenth-century depictions of the interior. "The novel" she writes:

> for a long while, has been over-furnished. The property man has been too busy about the pages, the importance of material objects and their vivid presentation have been so stressed, that we take for granted whoever can observe, and can write the English language, can write a novel. Often the latter qualification is considered unnecessary. (Cather 1936:47)

Observation, is apparently, according to Cather, more valued than writing. Whilst bemoaning the extent and level of detail of description, she nevertheless maintains the metaphor, at the end of the essay calling for a return to "drama and four walls." When, one might ask, did fiction become a house?

In thinking about the relationship between the novel and the domestic interior, and trying to unpick this metaphor of "the house of fiction," a series of questions occurs. Can we identify specific reasons why the interior plays such an important role in the novel? Is there something particular about the changing depictions of interiors in fiction of the period 1720–1920 that might not be true of other subjects of representation? In other words, is there a particular affinity between the novel and the house—is the novel the natural home for literary representations of the home, or is the resonance of James's phrase merely fortuitous?

Two related metaphors are similarly intriguing. If fiction figures as a house, then its interior frequently figures interiority. Again, is this more than linguistic felicity? The association between the representation in fiction of a character's internal mental state, self-awareness or interiority, and a focus on the interior, specifically the domestic interior, appears pervasive and sustained. Historian John Lukacs claims that "The interior furniture of houses appeared together with the interior furniture of minds" (Lukacs 1970: 623). This assertion is corroborated, according to Lukacs, by the fact that a whole series of words denoting "the interior landscape" of our minds appeared in roughly the same period as an increase in the furnishings of the interior:

> Words such as self-love, self-confidence, self-command, self-esteem, self-knowledge, self-pity; other words such as disposition, character, ego, egoism, conscience, melancholy, apathy, agitation, embarrassment, sensible, sentimental appeared in English or French in their modern sense only two or three hundred years ago. And as their appearance marked the emergence of something new in the minds of peoples, something new appeared, too, in their daily lives. As the self-consciousness of medieval people was spare, the interiors of their houses were bare, including the halls of nobles and of kings. (Lukacs 1970: 623)

Medieval scholars might contest both Lukacs' characterization of medieval interiors, and the assumption of a lack of self-consciousness before the vocabulary he points to. The time period he suggests might also seem rather vague, but it is irrefutable that there are important shifts in the imagining of the home, of ideas of privacy, comfort, and the differentiation of room use, between 1400 and 1700, and that there is, broadly, a series of linguistic tropes which link the domestic interior and its furniture to the interior of the mind (Rybcznski 1986).

The associated metaphor of "mental furniture" occurs across disciplines, and across time. Swift's poem "The Furniture of a Woman's Mind" dates from 1727 but uses "furniture" to mean that which fills the mind, and makes no reference to actual furniture. Elsewhere Swift catalogues the objects of an interior to suggest men's (or more frequently women's) physical and mental states. His scatological poem "The Lady's Dressing Room" (1732) offers "a strict survey" through the eyes of Celia's lover Strephon whose "inventory" catalogues the horrors visual, tactile and olfactory of his beloved's dressing room, such as the "Handkerchiefs forgot/All varnish'd o'er with snuff and snot" and stockings "stained with the marks of stinking toes" (Swift 1732: II 49–52). We don't have to go far into Freud's work either on dreams or on language to find this association operating very powerfully. In the essay quoted above, Willa Cather allows that Tolstoi's depictions of the interior, for example in such novels as *War and Peace* (1863–9) and *Anna Karenina* (1873–7), achieve this crucial fusion at a narrative level: "the clothes, the dishes, the haunting interiors of those old Moscow houses are always so much a part of the emotions of the people that they are perfectly synthesized; they seem to exist not so much in the author's mind as in the emotional penumbra of the characters themselves" (Cather 1936: 52).

For Cather, this synthesis is one feature which distinguishes "the novel as a form of amusement," albeit "a vivid and brilliant form of journalism" from "the novel as a form of art." In 1936 the future of fiction lay for Cather not in verisimilitude, but in simplification:

"following the development of modern painting [...] to present the scene by suggestion rather than by enumeration." Cather, with her plea to "throw all the furniture out of the window, and along with it, all the meaningless reiterations concerning physical sensations" (Cather 1936: 55) advocates a turn from the enumeration of objects and the evidence of the senses towards abstraction. Her essay, looking back from the 1930s over two centuries of the novel, simultaneously acknowledges and rejects the centrality of literal descriptions, arguing instead for a return, on behalf of the reader as much the writer, to the power of imagination, another form of synthesis of mind and matter, which seems to have particular resonance in the evocation of the domestic interior.

If we look at the etymology of the word "interior," dating, according to the OED from 1490, it is clear that its earliest meanings relate to the mental, appearing as a synonym for "inward" in 1513. References to the interior meaning "inland" occur from the 1770s; the OED cites meanings referring to the inside of a building or room, or "a picture or representation" from the 1820s. At around this date the interior is established as itself a subject, rather than context, in visual representations. But what of novelistic depictions of the interior, when does the shift from context to subject occur? Can we identify specific moments of change or is this a history of repeated, overlapping and recurring shifts?

Of the various accounts of the growth of the British novel, one of the earliest, Ian Watt's *The Rise of the Novel* (1957), is still influential. Watt argues for what he terms "formal realism" as the defining characteristic of the new type of fiction produced by, initially, Daniel Defoe, Samuel Richardson and Henry Fielding. Watt turns to philosophy for an adequate definition of realism, and notes that "modern realism, of course, begins from the position that truth can be discovered by the individual through his senses: it has its origins in Descartes and Locke, and received its first full formulation by Thomas Reid in the middle of the eighteenth century." Watt talks about "the concept of realistic particularity" and states: "two [...] aspects suggest themselves as of especial importance in the novel—characterisation and presentation of background."(Watt 1957: 26).

In this light, if we accept Watt's version of the development of realism in the novel being linked to the empiricist philosophy of Locke and Reid, it is not surprising that authors give us increasingly detailed descriptions of their protagonists' material culture. In, for example, Daniel Defoe's, *A True Relation of the Apparition of One Mrs Veal* (1706), Defoe's persuasive retelling of a ghost story, several of his many authenticating devices evoke his characters' immediate material surroundings. As the ghostly Mrs. Veal "who was in a Riding Habit" arrives, "the clock struck Twelve at Noon." Later Mrs. Veal tells Mrs. Bargrave that her "Gown sleeve" is "a Scower'd Silk, and newly made up." (Defoe 1968: 137). However, neither in this short narrative, nor in Defoe's extended fiction do we get a sustained sense of the rooms or houses in which action takes place. According to Watt, "Defoe would seem to be the first of our writers who visualized the whole of his narrative as though it occurred in an actual physical environment," but acknowledges that "this solidity of setting is particularly noticeable in Defoe's treatment of moveable objects in the physical world." (Watt 1957: 26).

Robinson Crusoe describes building his house and his "castle," but our sense of those spaces derives from the objects in them. Similarly in *Moll Flanders* (1722), the narrative dwells more on the articles of plate and fabrics Moll acquires, and the streets through which she flees her pursuers, than the spaces she inhabits. In *A Journal of the Plague Year* from the same year, and in his later *Roxana* (1724), Defoe again evokes rather than describes spaces. Roxana's dress is described in detail, whether it is the elaborate masquerade costume, which gives her and the novel its name, or her Quaker dress. Defoe lingers on her clothes and other portable personal objects, which constitute her fortune, rather than her surroundings. Much of the action in the central section of the novel takes place in a "good House, and well-furnish'd" (Defoe 1996: 212) belonging to a Quaker woman "in a Court in the Minories" (Defoe 1996: 210) (a street near the Tower of London) where Roxana secretes herself after leaving her glamorous but dissolute West End life. We get some sense of the lay-out of the house, as when Roxana, who has been sitting in her landlady's "Chamber up-stairs" tells us "I went down a Pair of Back-stairs with her, and into a Dining-Room, next to the Parlour in which he was" (Defoe 1996: 223), a room already described as "a very handsome Parlour below-stairs"(Defoe 1996: 221). Such moments, whilst recording use and movement through the house, do little to relate the characters to their surroundings.

The depiction of objects seems to be characteristic of realism from Defoe onwards. But the effect is not simple. Roland Barthes, describing a passage from Flaubert in his essay on "The Reality Effect" describes such details as apparently "futile;" from the point of view of structural analysis they "correspond to a kind of narrative luxury." For Barthes, the "concrete detail" is constituted by the direct collusion of "a referent and a signifier:"

> Just when these details are reputed to denote the real directly, all that they do—without saying so—is signify it; Flaubert's barometer, Michelet's little door finally say nothing but this: we are the real [...] the reality effect is produced, the basis of that unavowed verisimilitude which forms the aesthetic for all the standard works of modernity. (Barthes 1989: 148)

In depictions of the interior, the drive to represent the real is paralleled by a desire for insight into characters' minds, the synthesis which makes the difference for Cather. At what point are descriptions of the domestic interior identified with character? Samuel Richardson's epistolary narratives of the 1740s and 50s identify individuals closely with their surroundings. Richardson offers a new level of detail and intensity to his descriptions of the interior in both *Pamela* (1742) and *Clarissa* (1747–9), and depictions of the interior are increasingly freighted through his work (Wall 2004: 118-120; Lipsedge 2006). The house carries important ideological weight in the battles over Richardson's female characters' lives. Pamela is a lady's maid whose mistress dies and whose new master, the lady's son, attempts to seduce her. She foils him and through maintaining her virtue against the odds, reforms and marries him. Her story is thus intimately related to the house, to domestic labor and domestic duty, and to the complex hierarchy of spaces in the mid eighteenth-century wealthy home. The little read second volume, much of it narrated through Pamela's journal, records the trials and tribulations of her married life, providing a detailed account of household management and domestic duty. Richardson's male protagonists' struggles over the female bodies they desire are mapped onto the intimate details of the domestic interior. These are domestic dramas and depend on the evocation of domestic space. These spaces are intrinsically hierarchical: library, closet, bed-chamber, dining room, summer house, all suggest particular modes of behavior which Richardson frequently has his protagonists transgress to dramatic effect.

Richardson's fictions were hugely popular, and strove through their appeal to a morality grounded in the evocation of feeling, to distance themselves from the scandal literature which preceded them. Depictions of interiors, especially scenes of seduction, had featured in the scandalous Restoration narratives by Delariviere Manly and Eliza Haywood (Ballaster: 1992). Richardson, a publisher as well as writer, took pains to distinguish his ostensibly moral narratives from such scandalous predecessors, adopting the term "history" rather than "novel." His writing practice reveals him to have been very conscious of his readership, gathering a group of virtuous group of female acquaintance around him who commented on *Clarissa* as it was written (Eaves and Kimple 1971, Eagleton 1982, Keymer: 1992).

By what point has the identification of character and interior seen in Richardson become a narrative given? It is clear if we look at the interiors described by Austen in *Mansfield Park* (1814) that they are of considerable significance. The sparse but distinct details of furnishings in Fanny's East Room suggest contemporary aesthetics, the taste for the picturesque, and Fanny's place in the family pecking order, as well as her own values.

> The comfort of it in her hours of leisure was extreme. She could go there after any thing unpleasant below, and find immediate

This is the true nature of home—it is the place of Peace; the shelter, not only from all injury, but from all terror, doubt and division. In so far as it is not this, it is not home; so far as the anxieties of the outer life penetrate into it, and the inconsistently-minded, unknown, unloved, or hostile society of the outer world is allowed by either husband or wife to cross the threshold, it ceases to be home; it is then only a part of that outer world which you have roofed over and lighted fire in. But so far as it is a sacred place, a vestal temple, a temple of the hearth watched over by Household Gods, before whose faces none may come but those whom they can receive with love,—so far as it is this, and roof and fire are types duly of a nobler shade and light,—shade as of the rock in a weary land, and light as of the Pharos in the stormy sea;—so far it vindicates the name, and fulfils the praise of Home. (Ruskin 2002; Grant 1984: 88)

Few of the homes Dickens portrays, whether loveless or loving, conform to Ruskin's radical disjunction between the "outer world" and the interior, except perhaps Wemmick's fortified castle in *Great Expectations,* and, as we've seen, Dickens relishes a nightmarish vision of the home in the same novel. Ruskin renders his interior sacred, its physical characteristics of roof and hearth elevated to ideal and symbolic function. Whilst Ruskin's description is clearly highly mediated and determined by a very specific cultural moment, his vocabulary grounds his view in the authority of a classical past through reducing the idea of home to its central metonymic components of "roof" and "hearth." His idealization, which enlists classical authority and the "Household Gods," simultaneously evokes a Biblical, and by implication, Christian, world view, where "roof and fire" are "types" of "a nobler shade and light."

Not only is the depiction of domestic interiors central to Dickens' novels' concerns with the related themes of home and childhood, which are such an important part of the enduring legacy of his fiction, but the ways in which his novels were circulated and read also tells us a lot about how the home was conceived of in the period. Many of Dickens' mature novels were published in serial form, either weekly or monthly, and the complete novel published to coincide with the final issue, for example, the first issue of *Great Expectations,* appeared in December 1860 in *All Year Round*, the magazine Dickens edited and published from 1859.

In his later years, Dickens became famous for his live readings from his novels, but the model of serial publication remained key to both composition and reception of his fiction. And serial publication has, as Dickens was keen to emphasize, a very particular and immediate relationship to its reading audience. Whilst early serial publications such Joseph Addison and Richard Steele's *The Spectator* (1711–12) saw their audience as occupying a public reading space, specifically the coffee house, Dickens' rhetorical strategy is to imagine his readers at home. From 1850 until its incorporation into *All Year Round*, he edited *Household Words* in which serialized fiction appeared including his own; for example *Hard Times* appeared weekly in 1854, and was then published in book form in the same year. *Household Words* described itself as "the gentle mouthpiece of reform;" Dickens termed himself its "Conductor," and led a sustained attack on current social abuses, crusading on behalf of education, sanitary reform, prison reform, decent houses for the poor, and safety in factories. (Grant 1984: 40).

The best known example of Dickens' reading public's response to his fiction is perhaps the reception of the death of Little Nell in *The Old Curiosity Shop* (1840). That he is well aware of his readers' responses to his writing, and saw his role as a writer as reflecting both his public and his private life is reflected in his extraordinary denial of wrongdoing concerning his separation from his wife Catherine in a statement which occupied the front page of the June 12, 1858 edition of *Household Words*. Headed simply "Personal" Dickens states that "Three and twenty years have passed since I entered into my present relations with the Public [...] through all that time I have tried to be as faithful to the Public, as they have been to me." He goes on to acknowledge that "some domestic trouble of mine [...] of a sacredly private nature," (the breakdown of his marriage), has caused him to "deviate from the principle I have so long observed, by presenting myself in my own Journal in my own private character, and entreating my brethren [...] to lend their aid to the dissemination of my present words." The piece never actually states what Dickens has been accused of, but in a strange blend of revelation and concealment attempts simultaneously to give his readers access to the "sacredly private" by "circulating the Truth" and to prevent further speculation.

This somewhat unwelcome public access into the writer's private life follows the rethinking of the public status of the domestic evidenced by the Matrimonial Causes Act of 1857, and the establishment in 1858 of a divorce court dedicated to dealing with matrimonial law. In the aftermath of this legislation and the social changes it implies came a series of novels of sensation in which the domestic interior is explored and the integrity of private rooms violated. The most telling example is perhaps Mary Elizabeth Braddon's *Lady Audley's Secret* (1862) in which Lady Audley's secret passageway is discovered and her chamber broached and ransacked.

One simple explanation for the amount of work descriptions of the domestic interior can do in fiction might relate to the many different narrative styles available to the novelist. And those narrative modes which exploit the association between the interior and the viewing subject's interiority are especially fruitful. It is of course, not merely that descriptions tell us about a character's environment, and by extension, socio-economic status and aesthetic concerns, it is, as I've suggested, a spectacularly rich vein for revealing a protagonist's response to others. In Dickens' *Little Dorrit* (1755–7), we see Mrs. Clennam's house through the eyes of both Little Dorrit, the maid coming to the big house to sew, and Arthur Clennam, the hen-pecked son returning from twenty years in China. The house, central to the plot, collapses in the course of the narrative, but until that point acts as a focus of different characters' experiences. Arthur finds the house dark, lugubrious, imposing, stifling and confining. Walking up through the "old close house" Arthur comes to a large garrett bedroom described as "Meagre and spare, like all the other rooms, it was even uglier and grimmer than the rest" (Dickens 1998: 49). Little Dorrit, brought up in the Marshalsea prison for debtors, finds the house brighter and less stuffy than Arthur. We not only get a rich image of an interior from two perspectives, we also get an insight into those characters and their experiences. And the novel is, as a genre, as I've already suggested, spectacularly good at revealing both action and thought, and conveying experience across time. If we look again at Dickens' narrative style in the above passage, we see it follows closely the thoughts and speech patterns of his characters. In the opening of Chapter Fourteen, Dickens makes the identity of his viewpoint explicit:

> This history must sometimes see with Little Dorrit's eyes [...] Little Dorrit looked into a dim room, which seemed a spacious one to her, and grandly furnished. Courtly ideas of Covent Garden, as a place with famous coffee-houses, where gentlemen wearing gold-laced coats and sword had quarrelled and fought duels; costly ideas of Covent Garden [...] all confused together,—made the room dimmer than it was, in Little Dorrit's eyes, as they timidly saw it from the door. (Dickens 1998: 167–8)

Free indirect discourse, or style, is the term given to that type of third person narration which takes the linguistic characteristics of the perceiving character. Associated with, amongst others, Jane Austen and Gustav Flaubert, it is a highly appropriate mode for the description of interiors. Returning to the description of Fanny Price's East Room in *Mansfield Park*, for example, Austen's observing eye and language are those of her heroine:

> To this nest of comforts Fanny now walked down to try its influence on an agitated, doubting spirit—to see if by looking at Edmund's profile she could catch any of his counsel, or by giving air to her geraniums she might inhale a breeze of mental strength herself. But she had more than fears of her own

> perseverance to remove; she had begun to feel undecided as to what she *ought to do*; and as she walked round the room her doubts were increasing. Was she *right* in refusing what was so warmly asked, so strongly wished for? (Austen 1980: 174)

Here Austen follows Fanny's thought patterns in relation to what she sees in her room. This type of narrative has its logical endpoint in modernist explorations of style in the early twentieth century by, amongst others, James Joyce, Virginia Woolf, and Dorothy Richardson characterized, not entirely satisfactorily, under the phrase "stream of consciousness." In Woolf's celebrated evocation of the Ramseys' summer house in *To The Lighthouse* (1927) we are taken on a mental tour of the house, her concerns about its inhabitants and her own life, by Mrs. Ramsey as she tries to measure her son's leg in order to take clothes to the lighthouse keeper's children.

> She looked up—what demon possessed him, her youngest, her cherished?—and saw the room, saw the chairs, thought them fearfully shabby. Their entrails, as Andrew said the other day, were all over the floor; but then what was the point; she asked herself, of buying good chairs to let them spoil up here all through the winter when the house, with only one old woman to see to it, positively dripped with wet? (Woolf 1992: 38)

The success of free indirect discourse, and stream of consciousness, together with the other narrative options of first- and third-person narration, give us one possible answer to some of my opening questions. The association of home and character may, by the end of the nineteenth century, be a novelistic, even a cultural, given, and one consciously expounded by the cynical, materialistic and manipulative Madame Merle in *The Portrait of a Lady*.

> When you've lived as long as I you'll see that every human being has his shell and that you must take the shell into account. By shell I mean the whole envelope of circumstances. There's no such thing as an isolated man or woman; we're each of us made up of some cluster of appurtenances. What shall we call our "self'? Where does it begin? Where does it end? It overflows into everything that belongs to us—and then it flows back again. I know a large part of myself is in the clothes I choose to wear. I've a great respect for *things*! One's self, and one's house, one's furniture, one's garments, the books one reads, the company one keeps—these things are all expressive. (James 1995: 222–223)

It is, however, the author's internalization of those associations through the structures of narrative which makes depictions of the interior such a powerful novelistic tool.

I would argue that the multiple narrative voices available to the novelist, and, in particular the techniques of free indirect style and stream of consciousness allow for exceptionally engaged depictions of the domestic interior. These depictions reveal for the reader the processes of that other, older version of the interior, the mind. Thus as descriptions move from object to interior, from Defoe's focus on objects towards Woolf's evocation of an interior, via the nineteenth century's fascination with the minutia of domestic interiors, I would suggest that that shift is facilitated in part by changing narrative techniques. The novel's structural versatility allows the author to describe interiors through the characters' perceptions, and to engage in so doing with characters' pasts and futures in a way which is difficult in other media. These narrative modes are of course available (and used) in describing other scenes and locations. However, particularly in novels which focus on women's experience, houses often play a key role in the narrative, and serve as indicators of past experience (childhood, for example) as well as offering clues to a series of potential futures.

There does seem to be an affinity between the novel and the house, and the novel, through its formal qualities and distinctive narrative techniques is one very successful home for literary representations of the home. The "house of fiction" proves not to be an empty metaphor, rather a complex and suggestive image which reflects the multiplicity of different engagements of the novel with representations of the domestic interior. This extended period of the novel's development broadly sees a shift from the depiction of objects and experience in a search for the truth offered by realism to the inclusion of detailed depictions of the interior as the norm and towards a return to abstraction. In each era, the search to represent psychological truth, or interiority, seems in these narratives, bound up with depictions of the interior, a critical fusion achieved through the narrative techniques of free indirect style and stream of consciousness.

REFERENCES

Austen, Jane. 1980. *Mansfield Park*, first published 1814, edited by Tony Tanner. Harmondsworth: Penguin.

——. 1996. *Pride and Prejudice*, first published 1813, edited by Vivien Jones. Harmondsworth: Penguin.

Ballaster, Ros. 1992. *Seductive Forms: Women's Amatory Fiction from 1684–1740*. Oxford: Clarendon Press; New York: Oxford University Press.

Barthes, Roland. 1989. *The Rustle of Language*, translated by Richard Howard. Berkley and Los Angeles: University of California Press.

Cather, Willa. 1936. "The Novel Démeublé," in *Not Under Forty*, pp. 47–56. London, Toronto, Melbourne and Sydney: Cassell and Co.

Defoe, Daniel. 1968. "A True Relation of the Apparition of One Mrs Veal," first published 1706, in *Robinson Crusoe and other Writings*, edited by James Sutherland. pp. 134–141. Boston: Houghton Mufflin,

———. 1996. *Roxana*, first published 1724, edited by John Mullan. Oxford: Oxford University Press.

Dickens, Charles. 1977. *Great Expectations*, first published 1861, edited by Angus Calder. Harmondsworth: Penguin, 1977.

———. 1998. *Little Dorrit*, first published 1861, edited by Stephen Wall and Helen Small. London: Penguin.

Eagleton, Terry. 1982. *The Rape of Clarissa: Writing, Sexuality and Class Struggle in Samuel Richardson*. Minneapolis: University of Minnesota Press.

Eaves, T.C. Duncan and Ben Kimple. 1971. *Samuel Richardson, a Biography*. Oxford: Oxford University Press.

Eliot, George. 1965. *Middlemarch: A Story of Provincial Life*, first published 1871–2. Harmondsworth: Penguin.

Finn, Margot. 2002. "The Novel and the Romantic Domestic Interior: Negotiating National Identity in England and the Celtic Fringe" paper presented at CSDI Symposium: Representing the Domestic Interior: 1400 to the Present. Victoria and Albert Museum, 24–25 May.

Grant, Allan. 1984. *A Preface to Dickens*. London and New York: Longman.

James, Henry. 1995. *The Portrait of a Lady*, first published 1881, edited by Nicola Bradbury. Oxford: Oxford University Press.

Keymer, Tom. 1992. *Richardson's Clarissa and the Eighteenth-Century Reader*. Cambridge: Cambridge University Press.

Lipsedge, Karen. 2006. "Enter into thy closet" in John Styles and Amanda Vickery (eds) *Gender, Taste and Material Culture in Britain and North America in the Long Eighteenth Century*. Newhaven and London: Yale Centre for British Art, Yale University Press, forthcoming.

Lukacs, John.1970. "The Bourgeois Interior," *American Scholar* 39(4): 616–630.

Ruskin. John. 2002. "Lecture II. Of Queens' Gardens, Section 68". *Sesame and Lilies*. Edited by Deborah Epstein Nord. Yale University Press New Haven, CT.

Rybcznski, Witold. 1986. *Home: A Short History of an Idea*. New York: Viking.

Swift, Jonathon. 1732. *The Lady's Dressing Room*. London: J. Roberts.

Wall, Cynthia. 2004. "A Geography of Georgian Narrative Space" in Miles Ogborn and Charles W.J. Withers (eds) *Georgian Geographies: Essays on Space, Place and Landscape in the Eighteenth Century*, pp.114–129. Manchester and New York: Manchester University Press.

Watt, Ian 1957. *The Rise of the Novel*. London: Hogarth Press.

Woolf, Virginia. 1992. *To the Lighthouse*, first published 1927, edited by Margaret Drabble. Oxford: Oxford University Press.

MORAG SHIACH

MODERNISM, THE CITY AND THE "DOMESTIC INTERIOR"

MORAG SHIACH IS VICE PRINCIPAL (TEACHING AND LEARNING) AND PROFESSOR OF CULTURAL HISTORY IN THE SCHOOL OF ENGLISH AND DRAMA AT QUEEN MARY, UNIVERSITY OF LONDON. HER RECENT PUBLICATIONS INCLUDE *MODERNISM, LABOUR AND SELFHOOD IN BRITISH LITERATURE AND CULTURE, 1890–1930* (CAMBRIDGE UNIVERSITY PRESS, 2004) *AND FEMINISM AND CULTURAL STUDIES* (OXFORD UNIVERSITY PRESS, 1999).

This article argues that the overwhelming critical and historical focus on the figure of the *flâneur* in readings of literary modernism has led to the marginalization of key aspects of the experience of living and writing in the modern city: the marginalization, in fact, of the domestic interior. Having situated the reasons for the dominance of this critical paradigm, the article then explores whether we might be able to generate a comparably historicized cultural project, based on readings of Woolf, of Richardson, and of Pound and his circle, that engages with the more confined, and the more static terrain of the room as a way of reading the modern city. It analyzes some of modernism's key interiors, beginning with rooms in a number of Virginia Woolf's texts, and considering how they range of feminist critics since the 1980s. Thus, for example, Janet Wolff explored the extent to which this heroic figure of resistance to modernity was necessarily gendered, in her 1985 essay "The Invisible *Flâneuse*," which argued that attention to the gendered division of public and private spaces would suggest that a female *flâneur* always risked the wrong sort of visibility. But Wolff's caution about the relevance of the *flâneur* to a cultural history of women and modernity was not shared by all feminist critics. Rachel Bowlby responded to these critical questions in a series of influential readings of Virginia Woolf, which stressed the extent to which Woolf's writing explored and enacted the position of the *flâneuse*. Bowlby's position developed from her critical and historical interest in women as consumers in the modern city, first developed in her *Just Looking* (1985). Indeed, this interest in consumption might itself be understood in relation to a broader set of questions about political agency and activism within feminism, and the general Left, in the 1980s, and to the perceived need to turn attention from the structures of production to the processes of consumption in political analyses of the period.

Bowlby's readings of Woolf stressed the centrality of wandering London streets, both to the imagining of a modern femininity through a character such as the young Elizabeth Dalloway in *Mrs Dalloway*, and to the everyday structure of Woolf's writing life (Bowlby 1997). Woolf's essay, "Street Haunting" (1927) emerges as the privileged text in this analysis, because it articulates the fascination of London streets and the exhilaration of their random and anonymous encounters. "Street Haunting" becomes the figure for a type of *flânerie* that might be possible for women, as it articulates a movement from the domestic space to the various spaces of consumption offered by the modern city, dwelling on the role of fantasy in the unfolding of this kind of urban journey. The essay, and the activity of "street haunting" are also important in a text such as Jean Radford's *Dorothy Richardson*, where street haunting is the counterpoint to Radford's analysis of Richardson's uneasy relation to the family hearth, and by implication to domestic interiors (Radford 1991: 58ff.). The continuing reach and significance of Woolf's essay, and its impact on the cultural framework for the reading and interpretation of modernist writing, can perhaps be discerned in the decision of Penguin Books to publish it as one of their seventy "Pocket Penguins" which appeared in May 2005 in celebration of their seventieth anniversary.

Bowlby's reading of Woolf as *flâneuse* has been influential, both for the study of Virginia Woolf and more broadly for the critical reception of literary modernism. It has led to a range of critical work that addresses the relations between modernity and the city, which is understood primarily as a network of public spaces, usually of streets, and which is particularly interested in the subversive potential of walking in the city. Even when Bowlby turns her attention to a text such as *A Room of One's Own*, where the importance of interior space is so fully articulated, she is drawn to the walking and the mobility that structure the text as a whole (Bowlby 1997: 207). Disruption, creativity, and modern modes of femininity are all increasingly read in and through the possibilities of "street haunting," which seems to challenge boundaries and to refuse stasis. In similar ways, Dorothy Richardson's protagonist in *Pilgrimage*, Miriam Henderson, has been read as expressing the innovative, creative and transgressive potential of the modern city and its possible modes of subjectivity, in passages such as the following from "The Tunnel" (the fourth of the thirteen "novel-chapters," originally published in 1919):

> I'm free—I've got free—nothing can ever alter that, she thought. [...] A strength was piling up within her. She would go out unregretfully at closing time and up through unknown streets, not her own streets, till she found Holborn and then up and round through the squares. (Richardson 1979: II, 76–7)

But this critical recovery of the imaginative and subjective transgressions of *flânerie* has its blind-spots, and its emphasis on the relation of modernist writers to public spaces and to city streets can lead to an under-estimation of the ways in which the modernist city depends on, and also draws from, the domestic interior.

In the extensive critical literature of the *flâneur/flâneuse*, as we have seen above, we have a theoretical and critical landscape, in which it is possible to read walking through the city as part of a narrative of modernity, and to read modernist literature as a privileged site for the articulation of a resistant subjectivity. My aim, however, is now to explore whether we might generate a comparably historicized cultural project, based on readings of Woolf, of Richardson, and of Pound and his circle, that engages with the more confined, and the more static terrain of the room as a way of reading the modern city. The question is partly suggested by Woolf's choice of titles such as *Jacob's Room* or *A Room of One's Own* for her own published work, which suggest that both the semantic and the social boundaries of rooms were peculiarly important for her writing. It is also informed by recent critical work that seems to be moving towards the articulation of domestic interiors as part of the landscape of the modernist city and also as a crucial imaginative and social resource for modernist cultural production, including Elisabeth Bronfen's *Dorothy Richardson's Art of Memory: Space, Identity, Text* (1999), Christopher Reed's *Bloomsbury Rooms: Modernism, Subculture, and Domesticity* (2004) and Peter Brooker's *Bohemia in London: The Social Scene of Early Modernism* (2004).

In the rest of this article I will examine some of modernism's interiors, beginning with rooms in a number of Virginia Woolf's texts, and considering how they figure as a space of memory, as a framework for identities, and as a locus of security. I will concentrate in particular on rooms in Kensington, and in Bloomsbury, which have a persistent presence in her texts throughout Woolf's writing life. In my discussion of Dorothy Richardson, I will concentrate on the hierarchies of domestic spaces, on the relations between the boundaries of the self and the boundaries of the room, and on the troubling landscape of the suburban in her novel *Pilgrimage*. Finally, in examining the cultural milieu of Ezra Pound, I will consider how London interiors provide the physical and the metaphorical landscape for particular forms of modernist innovation in the early years of the twentieth century.

VIRGINIA WOOLF'S LONDON ROOMS

Virginia Woolf's biographers agree on the emotional and psychological importance of 22 Hyde Park Gate, the large but cramped house in Kensington in which she spent the early years of her life. Woolf returns to explore her memories of 22 Hyde Park Gate at a number of moments in her writing life, increasingly registering the details of its interior. While her early journal could barely manage to sketch these interior spaces, her later writings increasingly detail the rooms and their significance for her. In "22 Hyde Park Gate," a lecture by Woolf from the early 1920s, there is a very powerful description of the ways in which the organization of spaces at Hyde Park Gate could create a sense of secrecy, of guilt, or of fear, which is focused on boundaries and barriers between rooms:

> It is of the folding doors that I wish to speak. How could family life have been carried on without them? As soon dispense with water-closets or with bathrooms as with folding doors in a family of nine men and women. [...] Suddenly there would be a crisis—a servant dismissed, a lover rejected, pass books opened, or poor Mrs Tyndall who had lately poisoned her husband by mistake come for consolation. [...] Though dark and agitated on one side, the other side of the door, particularly on Sunday afternoons, was cheerful enough. (Woolf 1978a: 165)

In her essay on "Old Bloomsbury," Woolf also writes powerfully, and polemically, about the rooms she is leaving behind at Hyde Park Gate:

> It was a house of innumerable oddly shaped rooms built to accommodate not one family but three. [...] To house the lot of us, now a storey would be thrown out on top, now a dining room flung out at bottom. [...] Here then seventeen or eighteen people lived in small bedrooms with one bathroom and three water-closets between them. (Woolf 1978b: 184–5)

Woolf stresses the sense of isolation and separation generated by these cramped and crowded rooms, so far from the noise of traffic or from the accident of passers-by. But she also remembers the rooms in this house as "tangled and matted with emotion," noting that "the walls and the rooms had in sober truth been built to our shape. We had permeated the whole vast fabric [...] with our family history" (Woolf 1978b: 186). So here another layer is added to the psychological meanings of the rooms in Hyde Park Gate. They are small and uncomfortable, and generate unwelcome intimacies. Family life depends on boundaries that are always in fact permeable: those folding doors were clearly far from soundproof. There is a stifling sense of isolation, of being cut off from the energy of the modern city and encased in a constraining Victorian shell. But there is also a saturation of emotion through which space becomes history, so that Woolf insists she could "write a history of every mark and scratch in my room" (Woolf 1978b: 186).

Woolf's "A Sketch of the Past," a text that might indeed read as such a "history of every mark and scratch" was written nearly twenty years later than "22 Hyde Park Gate." It returns to these interior spaces and to the emotional and psychological significance of the house's different rooms. Woolf's spatial imagination is here more expansive, as she writes of "that great Cathedral space that was childhood" (Woolf 1978c: 94). The suggestion is of grandeur of scale and beauty of architecture. But the detail of the house consistently confounds this effort towards architectural generosity. Woolf notes that:

> two different ages confronted each other in the drawing room at Hyde Park Gate: the Victorian Age; and the Edwardian Age [...]. The cruel thing was that while we could see the future, we were completely in the power of the past. (Woolf 1978c: 147).

She writes of a house in which she was at times able to "escape the pressures of Victorian society" by reading, borrowing books from her father's very extensive library. But,

> the change would come in the afternoon. About 4.30 Victorian society exerted its pressure. Then we must be 'in'. For at 5 father must be given his tea, And we must be better dressed and tidier [...] we would have to sit at that table, she [Vanessa] or I, decently dressed, having nothing better to do, ready to talk. (Woolf 1978c: 149)

This sense of living in two different times, and of being two different people, is mapped by Woolf onto the geography of the house, She writes of 22 Hyde Park Gate that:

> the division in our life was curious. Downstairs there was pure convention: upstairs pure intellect. But there was no connection between them. (Woolf 1978a: 158)

Yet we cannot help but recognize that this memory must be false, because Woolf herself had to forge such connections continually, moving between these spaces and sustaining both her social and her intellectual life.

Woolf's move from Kensington to Bloomsbury following her father's death is represented by her as an opportunity to reconfigure the social and affective significance of domestic space. The room for which Woolf longed in Bloomsbury was one "with books and nothing else, where I can shut myself up:" in fact, a study (Woolf 1975–80: 147). This is an interestingly non-domestic kind of interior space, which provides a necessary complication of the perhaps too easy tendency to identify the interiors of houses with the idea of a "domestic interior." The domesticity of interiors was, in fact a recurring point of contention in this period. In an influential analysis of the various spaces in which women lived independently from the mid-nineteenth century, Martha Vicinus dwells on the efforts of women's colleges to make their educational spaces seem reassuringly domestic, arguing that:

> rituals of domesticity were clearly intended to reassure parents and the public (and the women themselves) that higher education would not cut them off from their peers and families. (Vicinus 1985: 143)

Here then we find evidence of working spaces being actively configured as more familiar domestic interiors to reduce the threatening associations of women's education and women's professional labor. By contrast, however, in an essay on the artist Gwen John and her relation to Paris, Janet Wolff argues for the significance of the fact that John's artistic representations of women in interior spaces intriguingly resist the domestic through their insistence on representing single women alone. Wolff acknowledges the importance of interiors for Gwen John, citing her remark in a letter to Rodin that "my room is so delicious after a whole day outside, it seems to me that I am not myself except in my room," but she also stresses the ways in which this interior could be fashioned as an artistic rather than a domestic space (Wolff 1994: 118).

The urgent need for a form of interiority that was not domestic can be found in a diverse range of texts from the modernist period. For example, in a recent study of utopian thinking in the twenties, the historian Sally Alexander draws attention to a fictional autobiography by Kathleen Woodward, entitled *Jipping Street* (1928). This text describes Woodward's working-class childhood in Bermondsey, and Alexander argues that Woodward's desire for a room of her own, so forcefully articulated in the text, was "a plea for escape from the claustrophobia, abjection and narrow-mindedness of poverty" and for an alternative to a physically burdensome and coercive mode of domesticity (Alexander 2000: 275). Christopher Reed, on the other hand, suggests that this desire for a room expresses a need to escape inherited modes of domesticity, and to find the space and the resources to create modernist rooms that will contain new familial and social groupings. While observing that the desire for a room of one's own was a fairly widespread one among Woolf's creative peers, Reed argues that a room could provide a pretext and an opportunity for remaking both the self and aspects of the social. Thus he notes Lytton Strachey writing to Duncan Grant in 1909 in the following terms: "Good God! To have a room of one's own with a real fire and books and tea and company, and no dinner bells and distractions and a little time for doing something! It's a wonderful vision" (Reed 1996: 147). Similarly, Reed notes that Vanessa Bell shared her sister Virginia's desire for a room of her own, citing the remark, which is recorded in Frances Spalding's *Vanessa Bell*, that:

> all that seemed to matter was that at last we were free, had rooms of our own and space in which to be alone or to work or to see our friends. Such things may come naturally to many of the present generation but to me at least in 1904 it was as if one had stepped suddenly into daylight from darkness. (Spalding 1983: 49)

Among these potentially non-domestic interiors, the study was a room with particular significance for intellectual women in this period. The classicist Jane Harrison's discussion of the factors inhibiting women's entry into specific branches of scholarship includes merciless mocking of the ways in which men might use the study as "a place inviolate, guarded by immemorial taboos" where "he wants to be by himself," but Harrison is not immune to the attractions of such seclusion. Admitting that she may violate codes of femininity ("I have known for a long time that I am no 'true woman'") she nonetheless suggests that one of the most significant "signs of the times is that woman is beginning to demand a study" (Harrison 1915: 128).

Winifred Holtby's 1932 biography of Virginia Woolf certainly demonstrates a particular interest in the material and psychic importance of the study in Woolf's house at 52 Tavistock Square:

> Mrs Woolf herself uses as a study an immense half-subterranean room behind the house, piled with books, parcels, packets of unbound volumes, and manuscripts for the press [...] The light penetrates wanly down between the high buildings overhead, as through deep waters, and noises from the outside world enter only in a subdued murmur, as from very far away. (Holtby 1932: 35)

The underwater quality of this space is strikingly described by Holtby: it is "subterranean," the light seems to have traveled through water, and the subdued murmur has more of the sea that the street about it. In creating this working space, Woolf is disrupting the ordering of space and the hierarchy of rooms that had dominated her early life. She introduces fluidity into the apparently static and bounded space of a room.

Indeed, fluidity is frequently evoked in Woolf's representations of Bloomsbury rooms. For example, she describes 46 Gordon Square, to which she moved in 1904 following the death of her father, as follows:

> it was astonishing to stand at the drawing room window and look into all those trees; the tree which shoots its branches up into the air and lets them fall in a shower; the tree which glistens after rain like the body of a seal [...] we decorated our walls with washes of plain distemper. We were full of experiments and reforms. (Woolf 1978: 187)

These reforms created new kinds of space, and new ways of looking, "things one had never seen in the darkness [...] shone out for the first time in the drawing-room at Gordon Square".

From rigidity to fluidity, and from darkness to light, is the narrative Woolf offers of her move from Kensington to Bloomsbury. This may seem like an easy tale of modernity achieved, but the fascination of the hidden, bounded, dark spaces of her childhood is not so easily written out. Looking across the range of Woolf's prose writings, we find the security of darkness and enclosure constantly struggling with the fascinations and the liberations associated with light, a dialectic famously expressed in the recurrent image of a moth heading inevitably, but also insistently, towards its own destructive flame.

DOROTHY RICHARDSON'S MODERNIST INTERIORS

Dorothy Richardson's modernist novel, *Pilgrimage* consists of thirteen "chapters," which are also intact novels, which collectively map the life of a modern woman from 1890 to 1914. This modern life is lived in relation to a number of semantically and affectively charged spaces, amongst the most significant of which are a number of London rooms. The novel's protagonist, Miriam Henderson's relations to work, to sexuality, and to the social are all worked through and represented in relation to interior spaces. *Pilgrimage* both begins and ends with Miriam reflecting on the significance of her room, and measuring her sense of her self against its boundaries. Thus in the first novel-chapter, "Pointed Roofs" we read:

> Miriam left the gaslit hall and went slowly upstairs. The March twilight lay upon the buildings, but the staircase was almost

dark. The top landing was quite dark and silent. There was no one about. It would be quiet in her room. She could sit by the fire and be quiet and think things over. (Richardson 1979: I, 15)

Going upstairs is here a matter of entering a space that is private and reflective, qualities enhanced by the association of Miriam's room with darkness and silence. Similarly, very near the end of the final novel-chapter, "March Moonlight" we find Miriam once more seeking solitude and self-confirmation within the bounded space of her own room:

No one in the other room of this top floor. The garden, its washing lines, ash-heap and dustbins invisible from where I sit alone with the sky, the lime tree and the tops of those poplars pointing up in the next garden.
Solitude. Secure. Filled each morning with treasure undamaged by compulsory interchange. (Richardson 1979: IV, 655-6)

That final phrase, "treasure undamaged by compulsory interchange," powerfully evokes the damage that might be caused by undesired and uncontrollable forms of social interaction and also celebrates the role of the room as a protective barrier to such coercive sociability. Miriam's articulation of this secure solitude in her room seems to offer some kind of alternative to the *flâneur*'s fascination with transient and anonymous urban encounters, which has been so systematically offered as an authentic modernist subjectivity. Miriam Henderson's aspiration is for protection from the coerced and the casual encounter, a protection she represents here as the "treasure" of security.

The desire for protective boundaries finds expression throughout the text, and is articulated through the precise details of Miriam's domestic interiors. Boundaries can, of course, also be their own form of coercion, and the novel sequence is meticulous in its recording of the different modes of dependence and of independence that are possible in different domestic interiors. The following passage from "The Tunnel" is a good example of how the material details of Miriam's rooms are interwoven with her project of writing a distinctive, and distinctively modern, subjectivity:

The bed, drawn in under the slope, showed an expanse of greyish white counterpane, the carpet was colourless in the gloom. She opened the door. Silence came in from the landing. The blue and gold had gone from the skylight. Its sharp grey light shone in over the dim colours of the thread-bare carpet and on to the black bars of the little grate and the little strip of tarnished yellow-grained mantelpiece, running along to the bedhead where a small globeless gas bracket stuck out at an angle over the head of the bed

[...] Twenty-one and only one room to hold the richly renewed consciousness, and a living to earn, but the self that was with her in the room was the untouched tireless self of her seventeenth year and all the earlier time. The familiar light moved within the twilight, the old light [...] She might as well wash the grime from her wrists and hands. (Richardson 1979: II, 14-16)

The meanness of the room does not render it inappropriate for Miriam's "richly renewed consciousness," but it does suggest the limits of this consciousness in its interaction with the world. For Jean Radford such meticulous description of interiors is part of Miriam's repudiation of the naturalness of the domestic and familial "hearth," which is literalized, and thus problematized through the careful and almost obsessive description of a series of different grates and fireplaces that are each precisely socially located and symbolically charged (Radford 1991: 51).

Miriam is aware throughout the novel that the separation she experiences in her various top-floor rooms is also a kind of marginalization, and we read in the earlier "Honeycomb," that "Presently she could, if she held firm, be alone, in a grey space inside this alien room, cold and lonely with the beginning of something [...] Downstairs, warmth and revelry"(Richardson 1979: I, 432). The division here echoes Woolf's representation of the hierarchy of spaces in her childhood home—and once more the sociability is experienced as coercive and is contrasted with the singular, but "firm" self of the upstairs room. Miriam Henderson has, in the end, a horror of domestic comfort, since it seems absolutely to express the threat of "compulsory interchange." For Miriam, this threat is at its greatest in suburban houses, which negate the possibility of separation and of the cold and lonely space that might be "the beginning of something." Suburban comfort is represented as the antithesis of the productive spaces of literary invention, which are bounded, separate, and lonely. Throughout *Pilgrimage* suburban rooms are narrative ends rather than beginnings, and not very happy ones. Domestic comfort is associated with enclosure, with the assumption of false versions of the self, and with the end of creativity. Miriam's preference from beginning to end is for urban interiors, in which she encounters "the old untouched freedom" in "undisturbed space, high above the quiet street" (Richardson 1979: IV, 185).

"EZRA LOOKED AFTER THE CAKES"

Ezra Pound moved to London in 1908 and quickly became a prominent figure within the cultural and social milieu of early modernism. Pound's childhood had been spent in a suburb of Philadelphia, and his response to the cultural significance of this suburban space resonates with the hostility to suburbia found in Richardson's *Pilgrimage*. He writes that "the suburb has no roots, no center of life" (Ackroyd 1980: 7), and in coming to London, Pound may in fact have been looking both for roots and a focus or center to his cultural and intellectual life. In the rest of this article, I will consider the role of the domestic interior in the construction both of such roots and of such a center for the cultural project of modernism as understood and created by Pound and his circle between 1908 and 1914.

On arrival in London, Pound first lived in Duchess Street, just off Portland Place in London W1 but, given his financial position, he quickly "moved to something cheaper and less comfortable in Islington in North London" (Stock 1970: 67). The privations of life in cheap accommodation in this period were acutely felt by Pound, and were vigorously articulated in an article in the *New Age* some years later, where he wrote of "bathrooms advertised to contain h. and c., in which only the cold tap worked, of 'pink, frilly paper decorations'" (Stock 1970: 67). By 1909 Pound was able to leave such uncomfortable, and distinctly unfitting, domestic space behind as he moved to a room at 10 Church Walk, Kensington, which was to be his main place of residence in London from then until his marriage in 1914. It is striking to note in what follows how very different Pound's Kensington was to the oppressive and coercive space imagined by Virginia Woolf.

Pound's room in Church Walk was on the first floor in a courtyard of small three-storied houses. The room:

> was simply furnished even after he added a few pieces of his own. There was an iron bed, a mahogany wash-stand that folded down to look like a desk, a "sort of iron armchair convertible to cot," cane chairs, and a small bath-tub that he pushed under the bed. (Stock 1970: 90)

This room clearly made a significant impression on those who visited it. Some fifteen years after Pound left this room, key aspects of the space and its furnishings appear in Richard Aldington's novel *Death of a Hero*. The character of Mr. Upjohn, whose habits so closely resemble those of Pound as he "irritatedly cast himself at full length upon a sofa, and spasmodically ate candied apricots" (Aldington 1929: 115), can be found in a room that shows just the disturbing tendency to conflate ablution and sociability found in the description of Pound's room above. George, the protagonist of Aldington's novel is "further gratified by being allowed to witness the strange and complex ablutions performed by Mr. Upjohn from a wash-basin startlingly concealed in a veneered mahogany tallboy" (Aldington 1929: 117).

From this room in Church Walk, Pound "sallied forth in his sombrero with all the arrogance of a young revolutionary poet" (Goldring 1943: 47) to develop his contacts and to promote the cause of his own poetic writing. The journeys Pound embarked on did include visits to the key public spaces of the London cultural avant-garde of this period, so powerfully evoked in Peter Brooker's recent study of *Bohemia in London*, including "The Cave of the Golden Calf," the Café Royal and the Eiffel Tower Restaurant. Yet Pound's London was also, strikingly, a network of domestic interiors. Much of his time was spent moving between the houses of influential allies such as Ford Madox Ford or W. B Yeats, generating the network of collaborative relationships that would ensure the publication and the critical dissemination of his poetic output. Pound writes that "I made my life in London by going to see Ford in the afternoons and Yeats in the evenings" (Tytell 1987: 51) and these visits take place in the private and domestic spaces of Ford's and Yeats's rooms.

Ford Madox Ford, novelist, essayist, and editor of the *English Review* was a key ally of Pound in these early years of the century. In 1908, Ford was living in a maisonette in Holland Park Avenue, which was later to become the editorial office of the *English Review*. This apartment was situated three stories above a poulterer and fishmonger's shop, and access to it was via a side door and up a dark flight of steps. This room was, apparently, "perpetually inundated with visitors" (Goldring 1943: 32). Ford's own account of this room casts Pound in a central but singular role:

> It was a rather handsome large drawing room in an old house. There were pictures by Pre-Raphaelites, old furniture, a rather wonderful carpet. The room was lit from both ends and L-shaped so that if you wanted a moment's private conversation with anyone you could go around the corner. Miss Thomas, large, very blonde and invariably good tempered, presided over the tea table. Ezra looked after the cakes. (Ford 1931: 308)

Pound, Ford tells us, was an enthusiastic consumer of these cakes, given to flinging himself into chairs, devouring huge quantities of pastries and reading out his own translations to the assembled company (Ford 1931: 291). There is a quality of excess in representations of Pound in this period, as he both dominates and subverts the contours of his domestic interiors. From 1910, Ford lived in South Lodge, a semi-detached villa in Campden Hill Road, Kensington, which belonged to his lover, Violet Hunt. Douglas Goldring argues that "the transformation of South Lodge from a rather stuffy and conventional Campden Hill villa, into a stomping ground for *les jeunes* was brought about more by Ezra Pound than by Ford," and suggested that Pound conducted himself here like a sort of "social master of ceremonies"

(Goldring 1943: 47). This dominance is also noted by Ford himself, who says of Pound that "in a very short time he had taken charge of me, the review, and finally of London" (Ford 1931: 291). But it is important to notice the significance here of Ezra and the cakes: presiding over the tea-table, flinging himself into chairs, declaiming his own verse, Pound manages to establish a cultural and a social authority that will underpin the project of taking charge of London.

This authority was also generated by his participation in W. B. Yeats's "Monday evenings." Yeats lived in two rooms, at 18 Woburn Buildings, Bloomsbury. Peter Brooker tells us that "Yeats's main room held a settle and a leather armchair, a chest containing his manuscripts, astrological papers and tarot cards, a table with two candlesticks, a bookcase with editions of Blake and William Morris" (Brooker 2004: 60). In this room Yeats regularly entertained poets, artists and critics with a mixture of readings and conversation. Goldring argues that "one of his [Pound's] greatest triumphs in London was the way in which he stormed 18 Woburn Buildings, the Celtic stronghold of W. B. Yeats, took charge of his famous "Mondays," precisely as he took charge of the South Lodge tennis parties" (Goldring 1943: 48). Other accounts talk of Pound taking charge of Yeats's wine and cigars and distributing them to the assembled company.

Pound's creation of his literary persona, his establishment of cultural authority, and his access to literary production were all negotiated within domestic spaces. Even when these domestic interiors had to some extent been re-made as "offices," like Ford's Holland Park maisonette, they retained their domestic associations with hospitality and sociability. There is little enough here of the need to repudiate the domestic through the construction of an alternative intellectual space of "the study" that we found among Woolf and her peers. Pound learned how to dominate these domestic interiors by assuming the role of host, serving the cakes and handing round the cigars, while he simultaneously constructed the intellectual and cultural networks that would sustain the forms of modernist cultural innovation to which he was most clearly committed. He was, in that sense, the poet of the domestic interior.

REFERENCES

Ackroyd, Peter. 1980. *Ezra Pound and His World*. London: Thames and Hudson.

Aldington, Richard. 1929. *Death of a Hero*. London: Hogarth Press (1984).

Alexander, Sally. 2000. "A Room of One's Own: 1920s Feminist Utopias." In *Women: A Cultural Review* 11(3), 273–288.

Benjamin, Walter. 1970. *Illuminations*. Edited by Hannah Arendt, translated by Harry Zohn; London: Jonathan Cape.

——. 1973. *Charles Baudelaire: A Lyric Poet in the Era of High Capitalist*. Translated by Harry Zohn; London: NLB.

Bowlby, Rachel. 1985. *Just Looking.* London: Methuen.

——. 1997. "Walking, Women and Writing." In *Feminist Destinations and Further Essays on Virginia Woolf.* Edinburgh: Edinburgh University Press.

Bronfen, Elisabeth. 1999. *Dorothy Richardson's Art of Memory: Space, Identity, Text.* Manchester: Manchester University Press.

Brooker, Peter. 2004. *Bohemia in London: The Social Scene of Early Modernism.* London: Palgrave Macmillan.

Certeau, Michel de. 1984. "Walking in the City." In *The Practice of Everyday Life*, pp. 91–110. Translated by Steven Rendall; Berkeley: University of California Press.

Ford, Ford Madox. 1931. *Return to Yesterday*. Edited by Bill Hutchings; Manchester: Carcanet (1999).

Goldring, Douglas. 1943. *South Lodge. Reminiscences of Violet Hunt, Ford Madox Ford and the "English Review" Circle.* London: Constable.

Harrison, Jane Ellen. 1915. "Scientiae Sacra Fames." In *Alpha and Omega*, pp. 116–142. London: Sidgwick and Jackson.

Holtby, Winifred. 1932. *Virginia Woolf.* London: Wishart.

Radford, Jean. 1991. *Dorothy Richardson.* London: Harvester Wheatsheaf.

Reed, Christopher. 1996. "'A Room of One's Own': The Bloomsbury Group's Creation of a Modernist Domesticity." In C. Reed (ed.), *Not at Home: The Suppression of Domesticity in Modern Art and Architecture*, pp. 147–160. London: Thames and Hudson.

——. 2004. *Bloomsbury Rooms: Modernism, Subculture, and Domesticity.* New Haven: Yale University Press.

Richardson, Dorothy. 1979. *Pilgrimage* (4 vols). London: Virago.

Spalding, Frances. 1983. *Vanessa Bell.* London: Weidenfeld and Nicolson.

Stock, Noel. 1970. *The Life of Ezra Pound*. Harmondsworth: Penguin (1985).

Tester, Keith (ed.). 1994. *The Flâneur.* London: Routledge.

Tytell, John. 1987. *Ezra Pound, the Solitary Volcano.* London: Bloomsbury.

Vicinus, Martha, 1985. *Independent Women: Work and Community for Single Women, 1850–1920.* London: Virago.

Wolff, Janet. 1985. "The Invisible *Flâneuse*: Women and the Literature of Modernity," *Theory, Culture and Society* 2(3): 37–48.

——. 1994. "The Artist and the Flâneur: Rodin, Rilke and Gwen John in Paris" in Keith Tester (ed.), *The Flâneur*, pp. 111–137 London: Routledge.

Woolf, Virginia. "Street Haunting" 1927, in Andrew McNeillie (ed.) *Essays of Virginia Woolf: Volume 4.* London: Hogarth Press, 1994.

——. 1978a. "22 Hyde Park Gate." In Jeanne Schulkind (ed.) *Moments of Being*, pp. 163–180. London: Grafton.

——. 1978b. "Old Bloomsbury." In Jeanne Schulkind (ed.) *Moments of Being*, pp. 181–207. London: Grafton.
——. 1978c. "A Sketch of the Past." In Jeanne Schulkind (ed.) *Moments of Being*, pp. 71–162. London: Grafton.
——. 1975–80. *Letters. Volume I: The Flight of the Mind, 1888–1912*. Edited by Nigel Nicolson and Joanne Trautman, (6 vols). London: Hogarth Press.

CATHERINE RICHARDSON
EARLY MODERN PLAYS AND DOMESTIC SPACES

CATHERINE RICHARDSON IS A LECTURER IN ENGLISH AND MODERN HISTORY AND FELLOW OF THE SHAKESPEARE INSTITUTE AT THE UNIVERSITY OF BIRMINGHAM. HER INTERDISCIPLINARY WORK FOCUSES ON THE SOCIAL, MORAL AND PERSONAL USES OF MATERIAL CULTURE. SHE HAS PUBLISHED ON THE MATERIAL COMPOSITION OF THE HOUSEHOLD, ON DOMESTIC TRAGEDY, AND ON THE SIGNIFICANCE OF CLOTHING IN EARLY MODERN SOCIETY.

This article investigates the representation of the domestic interior on the pre-Restoration English stage. It argues for the very specific nature of theatrical representations of the interior, and for a strong and meaningful connection between the household on and off the stage. Contrasting early modern representations with medieval and post-Restoration ones, it defines this period as uniquely interested in personal domestic space whilst employing no scenery with which to produce a sense of its enclosed nature. Within these constraints and possibilities, it is argued that the household is employed differently on stage within the genres of city comedy and domestic tragedy.

> How is it possible to represent a domestic interior on the stage? From the moment the English theatres were reopened at Charles II's Restoration to the throne in 1660, the answer to this question began to be obvious. You could use "scenes" or flats to suggest an indoor location, and you could produce the illusion of an interior space, one which was framed and separated from the audience by the proscenium arch which divided the fictional scene from the real time of the auditorium. In increasingly elaborate sets which aimed at mimetic representation, the domestic interior could eventually take on the full range of its extra-theatrical characteristics: it was enclosed, set apart, filled with properties which mimicked every kind of furniture. But from the establishment of the commercial theatre in the expanding metropolis of London in the second half of the sixteenth century, until all theatres were closed by order of parliament in 1642, the situation was very different.

This article focuses on the particular constraints and possibilities of that earlier period, and it therefore begins by analyzing the ways in which it was possible to represent space on the pre-Restoration stage, and considers them in relation to the social and political meanings of domestic life in early modern England. It historicizes, in other words, both halves of the term "domestic interior." However, although I am arguing that some specifically sixteenth- and seventeenth-century concerns shape the interpretation of all domestic representations, I also want to examine how such representations differ from one another as a result of the generic constraints of comedy and tragedy.

From 1609 onwards Shakespeare's company played in two different kinds of venue. In the summer they used the Globe on the south bank of the Thames, in the suburbs, outside the jurisdiction of the city. This massive amphitheatre could accommodate as many as 4,000 spectators, perhaps 1,000 of them standing in the yard and the rest seated in the tiered galleries around the outside of the "wooden O."[1] The stage jutted out into the yard and was reached by doors in the wall behind, and there may well have been a "discovery space" behind the stage too, an interior area in which people and props could be revealed by opening a door or drawing a curtain. Open to the elements, it was not possible to regulate stage light in an illusionistic way in such theatres, and the arrangement of actors and audience lent itself to interaction and metatheatrical contact.

In the winter, the King's Men left the cold of an open stage for the comparative comfort of their Blackfriars theatre, an indoor venue in a relatively small room of the old monastic complex on the north bank of the Thames. The stage was once more a thrust one, but in this venue the whole audience was seated, and the roofed space and artificial lighting lent themselves to a more intimate kind of performance. The wealthy patrons sat closest to the stage, but some of them also sat on it, and the action was therefore surrounded by its audience and tended towards a high level of interaction with them. In indoor venues, just as in their outdoor counterparts, actors and playwrights did not aim at the illusion of a reality separated off from the space of the spectators, and plays probably had to be flexible enough be staged in both types of playing space.

If the domestic interior had necessarily to be staged without the illusion of enclosed interior space, then it also had to be achieved on a famously "bare stage," without the need for elaborate scenery. The inventory of the Admiral's Men's props lists a "cloth of the sun and moon," and "the city of Rome," the closest approximations to what the post-Restoration commercial theatre might have thought of as scenery. "Rome" presumably offered a vista which represented the city as a whole, as a concept of "foreign location," and this is subtly different to an attempt to indicate a specific place within a city—the difference between place and space perhaps? The particulars of the space in which action took place on this stage, then, had to be indicated in some other way.

The list of props also includes a bedstead, and this offers our best evidence, outside the requirements indicated in the play texts themselves, of the physical ways in which an early modern domestic interior took shape. Textual requirements expand the picture: although the stage was bare of scenery, it was comparatively full of props, from small hand-props like napkins which might indicate that a character had entered from a meal imagined offstage (for instance *Enter Frankford as it were brushing the crumbs from his clothes with a napkin, and newly risen from supper* in scene VIII of *A Woman Killed with Kindness*), to large pieces of domestic furniture such as tables, chairs and beds which gave action a physical anchor on the otherwise markerless stage.[2]

Such props offered a crucial way of mediating between open space and this theatre's other most significant representational tool, the words which the actors spoke. Location came into being as the actors described it, and as they tied it to a particular part of the stage through their gestures. Alan Dessen has argued for the central importance of the small word "this" to pre-Restoration theatre practice, an economical way of anchoring description in the material properties of the actor's surroundings. But he goes further, suggesting a transformative role for stage gestures: "For the original spectator, the penthouse, bulk or hedge corner came into existence when the actor gestured towards something (a pillar, a railing) or some place, thus giving a local habitation and a name to an otherwise neutral area (a technique used many many times in this period to 'create' a city, a cave, a cell, walls, a tree, and more)"(Dessen 1984: 61). Using the features of the playing space and the props which were brought onto the stage, actors could temporarily alter the meaning of what the audience imagined, making the general specific for the duration of an exchange.

The advantage of such staging is, of course, that it is supremely flexible. What was "inside" a couple of minutes previously becomes "outside" as someone enters from somewhere else. This is a theatre in which space lacks physical stability. Because its character is formed through narrative and stage properties, spatial identity coheres around actors and objects; they bring its qualities into play by invoking the audience's imagination of space. Domestic location comes into place with them—around an intimate exchange or around a stool—and then it shifts when the mood is broken or the object removed, and "the domestic" dissipates instantly. In other words this kind of theatre often works against the *physical* aspects of space, which is in many ways reduced to a series of dynamics: the power relations between individuals; the significance of the street as opposed to the inn; the hovel in relation to the palace.

The representation of domestic interiors relies upon a limited but flexible series of forms. There are the rituals and processes of dining, with its connections to hospitality; there are rites of passage which focus around beds—childbeds and deathbeds. Interiors are suggested by the intersection of action with objects, then, by stools, tables or beds and the practices with which they are commonly associated. But interiors can also be indicated much more loosely, for instance by knocking off-stage, by entrances and welcomes, by characters being introduced onto the stage by servants. In these cases, space is only nominally interior, and the stage looks exactly the same as it would for an exterior scene.

The temptation is to regard this theatre as in some way under-developed, to think that the scenic developments of the next three centuries were aspects of performance which actors and playwrights would have embraced with open arms if only they had thought of them. The Victorian theatre attempted, in the words of Charles Kean's biographer "to place the poet [Shakespeare] on the stage for which he composed, to the best advantage, and *with the reality which he conceived and intended*, though without a hope of seeing the accomplishment with his own eyes" (quoted in Jackson 2001: 115; my italics) After all, these later developments grew out of royal and aristocratic entertainments which were contemporary to the plays considered here—out of the masques which used Inigo Jones's perspective-governed scenery, for instance. The accounts of royal entertainments show The King's Men performing *Henry V* at Whitehall on January 7th 1604–5, Ben Jonson's Masque of Blackness having been staged in the Banqueting House on the previous night (Streitberger 1986: 7). Such evidence demonstrates the habitual overlap of different kinds of entertainment for theatre professionals and their elite audiences, a cross-fertilization which makes its presence felt in, for instance, the masque in *Twelfth Night*.

But evolutionist understandings of early modern drama blatantly fly in the face of the textual evidence. The opening prologue to Shakespeare's *Henry V* celebrates the strikingly flexible nature of non-illusionistic representation in epic vein, as he begs for,

> a Muse of fire, that would ascend
> The brightest heaven of invention;
> A kingdom for a stage, princes to act
> And monarchs to behold the swelling scene! (1–4)[3]

He calls for a representation which transcends representation, which explodes the gap between a narrative about royal power and a stage of poor players by wishing that what is seen might actually *be* what is staged—a stage expanded physically to encompass the kingdom which it desires to represent. Such a representation would deny the point of theatre, which is to suggest things which are not there, and the prologue admits his hyperbole:

> But pardon, gentles all,
> The flat unraised spirits that hath dar'd
> On this unworthy scaffold to bring forth
> So great an object: can this cockpit hold
> The vasty fields of France? (8–12)

The answer is, of course, no. This is a problem of scale, he suggests, because France and Agincourt cannot ever be sufficiently represented on a stage. And it is for this reason that the actors must "On your imaginary forces work," encouraging the audience to "suppose," to "piece out," and to "think" because

> 'tis your thoughts that now must deck our kings,
> Carry them here and there, jumping o'er times,
> Turning th' accomplishment of many years
> Into an hour-glass (28–31)

As such a bold and witty opening speech makes clear, this was a theatre which derived amusement and great power from its "limitations"; within its disingenuous apology for physical inadequacy is a delight in the incredibly potent force of imagination. The comparative bareness of this stage, then, was celebrated as a fruitful conjunction of language and imagination which was never restricted by spatial visualizations.

This recognition of the centrality of the significant power of imagination to the construction of theatrical illusion had further consequences. With men playing the parts of women and commoners taking the part of kings, with lust, murder and sedition common narrative themes, the call to imagine, to complete a metonymic portrayal by "piecing it out" with one's own thoughts and ideas, was potentially seditious. Because theatre staged a whole range of politically and ideologically troubling subjects in this period, it provoked outspoken opinions from both its critics and its sponsors. They fully understood that it was a tool in the battle between good and evil over English souls, but whilst they agreed about its power they disagreed over whether it was an instrument wielded by man or by Satan. Francis Bacon, in his *Advancement of Learning* (1605), described the ways in which mass feeling rules audiences:

> play-going has been regarded by learned men and great philosophers as a kind of musician's bow by which men's minds may be played upon. And certainly it is most true, and one of the great secrets of nature, that the minds of men are more open to impressions and affections when many are gathered together than when they are alone. (Gurr 2004b: 121)

Theatre, then, is fundamentally different to private reading in the way it works upon the collective imagination, and the powerful "group-looking" which it demands alters the emotional engagement it offers, mitigating against a connection between interior space and a rapt interiority of reception by individual audience members.

Looking backwards rather than forwards in theatre history, it is clear that the status of domestic representation was strikingly different in this theatre. The two primary modes of medieval theatre, the mystery and morality plays, had represented Biblical narratives or abstract moral concepts around sin and repentance. But the early modern theatre was additionally interested in history, in both national history and personal history, and in histories of the development of mankind in "real time," not a time suspended loosely between creation and judgment. In other words, this new theatre was interested in *particularity*, the specifics of circumstance and individuality and their connections to action. And these differences affected the kind of space which the stage could signify. Mystery plays represented Biblical locations, such as the stable in which Mary gave birth to Jesus; morality plays used a richly complex symbolism of physical proximity and location—up and down, left and right—to express moral transformations as movements across the stage. But the early modern theatre wanted to be able to suggest Juliet's balcony; Richard II's "base court"; Dr Faustus' study. As commercial drama developed, playwrights became more adventurous with particularities of space and location.

Some general points about theatrical representations of the household pertain to all genres in this period. Firstly, this is not about *any* type of interior space: in particular, perhaps, the household is distinct from the inns which have a specific function in city comedies, where they are often paired with the bodies of whores as two types of space which *could* be exclusive and *could* employ a policy of restricted entry, but do not. Common to all representations of the household is its status as a repository for *unique familial* identity. The significance of this aspect of domestic space is easy to see in *The Comedy of Errors*, for instance, where one of the most disturbing aspects of the confusion between the identical twins Antipholus of Siracuse and Antipholus of Ephesus occurs when the former enters the latter's house. Everything contained within it, especially perhaps his brother's wife, was supposed to be specific to the householder, intended to reflect and shape his own identity. Implicit in this play is the fact that tying people to unique spaces makes them responsible, and it gives them identity. In contrast, Antipholus of Siracuse says, "I will go lose myself,/And wander up and down to view the city." Cities happen to people in early modern plays, they act upon them and change them. Houses form people, representing them to others and to themselves.

But if an argument about domestic spaces precludes discussion of inns, then it might not be about the kinds of interior space which offer a metaphor for individual mental interiority either. When the eponymous hero of Marlowe's *Dr Faustus* is discovered in his study, the audience is shown an interior, probably physically formed by the small discovery space at the back of the stage, whose bounded nature is a figure for male intellectual superiority and the power of the mind. Pedantically, studies may well be found within houses, but they are not governed by the particular dynamics of a patriarchal household, and they do not permit the representation of its function as a unit.

Indeed, the moral and political aspects of the household outside the theatre in this period are crucial, not only to the establishment of the topic of enquiry, but also to an understanding of the full range of its theatrical meanings. The household became central to the way in which social life was organized in early modern England because men and women lived in constant fear of communal disorder. The patriarchy to which they subscribed was the dominant mode of social organization because it was thought to be the most effective way of ensuring that someone was responsible for the behavior of each individual, and therefore had a vested interest in guaranteeing their peaceful conduct. This need for responsibility generated a focus on the dynamics of power—the relationship between those who were in authority and those who owed them obedience. In exploring these dynamics, early modern writers saw society as a series of related spheres, in which a man's control over his household was directly analogous to the magistrate's government of his community, and the king's command over the subjects of his realm. In the same way that living in England made individuals subject to her rules and her monarch, so living within the household made all its members subject to the wise rulership of its head. In order to avoid a universal anarchy, the *Homilie Agaynst Disobedience and Wylful Rebellion* stated, God had "ordayned that in families and housholdes, the wyfe shoulde be obedient unto her husbande, the children unto their parentes, the servantes unto their maisters"(1570, A2v).

Any concept of what we might think of as private life begins to disappear as "a conscionable performance of houshold duties, in regard of the end and fruit thereof, may be accounted a publike worke" (Gouge 1622: 18); there can be no works which are not public in their implications, *despite* their location, and all human activity must therefore be performed well and tend towards order. To guard against the dangers of weak domestic rule, early modern governors legitimized close observation of neighbors' domestic activity. Social, moral and spiritual order was therefore predicated upon denying the physicality of boundaries, upon legitimating their crossing as an absolute moral project of revelation to ensure stability. William Gouge suggests the implications of an analogical view of domestic order: "The honour and authority of God and of his son Christ Jesus is maintained in and by the honour and authority of a husband, as the King's authority is maintained by the authority of his Privy Council and other magistrates under him; yea, as an husband's authority is in the family maintained by the authority of his wife"(Gouge 1622: 468). While this casts the husband as a figure of Christ, it also gives a power to submission: the wife's actions in effect underpin the whole social order.

These political, social and moral implications must have affected the way audiences viewed domestic representations, and constrained the form those representations took. Arguably, these meanings were most pertinent and potent in relation to plays which made most insistent reference to contemporary social practice. The centrality of audience imagination suggests a scale of engagement which runs between memory and fantasy. On this scale, the expansion of representation's metonymy which audiences undertook when watching a scene set in Hamlet's castle must have been closer to fantasy than their "piecing out" of the antics in the Fords' house in *The Merry Wives of Windsor*, for instance. The two subgenres on which I focus here, city comedy and domestic tragedy, are perhaps the two most self-consciously mimetic forms of early modern drama, and as such they force their audiences to relate the representation they offer to domestic spaces outside the theatre. City comedies offer narratives of urban appetites. They have been said to be distinguished from other comedies: "by their critical and satiric design, their urban settings, [and] their exclusion of material appropriate to romance"(Gibbons 1980: 11). In other words they are interested in a form of realism: accurate depictions of the city for local interest, and of daily life in it for satirical purposes. Domestic tragedies often depict "true crime"—narratives of events whose didactic significance is inherent in the fact that they at least appear to have taken place within England's very recent past. They dramatize the specific circumstances, financial, sexual and interpersonal, which lead to adultery and murder within the household, and part of their appeal is the luridness of their reportage-like quality.

Both genres engage implicitly with the sociopolitical significance of domestic action. Satiric comedies comment on it ironically through characters like Allwit in *A Chaste Maid in Cheapside*, who runs his house "super efficiently" by letting Sir Walter Whorehound father his children and keep his family, thereby reneging all financial, social and even sexual responsibility (Middleton 1988). Domestic tragedies derive their compelling power from the disparity between the communal significance of domestic actions and their physical and psychological impenetrability within the house. Their narrative interest is in the failures of patriarchal rule and the monstrous crimes which take place as a result, and they often recognize the connections between gender and insubordination.

CITY COMEDY

Angela Stock and Anne-Julia Zwierlein list the "opposing, often contradictory forces" which city comedies dramatize: those "of tradition and novelty, participation and exclusivity, communal vision and social division, collective rites and private leisure, bounty and thrift"(Mehl *et al.* 2004: 18). These binaries flirt with the distinction between the city and the household, but in fact the satirical project of the plays ensures that the plots dramatize the way in which the other pairings cut across the physical boundaries between domestic and communal. It is rather the case that the household is incorporated into the representation of urban life, as a seamless part of its patterns of consumption and production. City comedies offer a world in which "identities, norms and rationality are pulled into the maelstrom of economic circulation" (Mehl *et al.* 2004: 18). The plays map models of commercial interaction onto social intercourse. As Pursenet explains in 3iii *Your Five Gallants* "the pocket keepes my boye, hee keepes me, I keepe her, shee keepes him, it runs like quick-siluer, from one to another"(1610–12). Antisocial behavior is synchronized by the rhythms of the city's commercial life, offering an immoral regularity. And just as it is impossible to keep anything personal, to keep it physically within the house (possessions, wives etc.), so it is impractical to keep out communal life, as becomes clear to Morose (a character who craves total silence within his house in the city) in his unsuccessful quest for a quiet life (Dutton 2003).

The plots of city comedies are only loosely causal, and the connections between their different strands are often linked to location: characters meet when going from street to street and are connected in ways which parody the notion of community—they share the same whores or try to marry the same people. The social diversity upon which satire feeds would not be available within a single household: the "distant knowledge" and slight acquaintance which provide the narrative dynamic for social difference and farcical humor can only be generated in the distinctions between households.

But although the household is given meaning by the impossibility of separating it fully from the streets of the town, these plays do stage complex representations of domestic interiors. One obvious example is *Volpone*, in which the eponymous character feigns near-death in order to provoke the generous ministrations of several individuals who hope to inherit his fortune. A large proportion of the play is therefore set in Volpone's bedchamber, where suitors to his wealth range around his bed offering gifts. Such scenes are socially self-selecting—only those of appropriate wealth can gain legitimate access (and they have to produce the material proof in the form of presents)—but they are therefore ripe grounds for social competition, always most acute amongst the *nearly* equal.

This type of representation is common to many types of play, where the bed itself produces intimate space by focusing the audience's attention. In 3ii *A Chaste Maid in Cheapside* the gossips gather in Mistress Allwit's lying-in chamber following the christening of her and Whorehound's latest child. They are all provided with "low stools" (7) around the bed, business which begins to suggest a bounded space on what remains an open stage. Allwit's comments following the departure of his wife's gossips further this impression by retrospectively insisting upon intimacy: "How hot they have made the room with their thick bums,/ Dost not feel it... How they have shuffled up the rushes too [...] With their short, figging, little shittle-cork heels!"(201–212). Here, the chamber becomes a space for outrageous female consumption, as the gossips devour as much of the wine and as many as possible of the celebratory sweetmeats provided by Whorehound. The concerns of the narrative characterize such physically intimate spaces as controllable, but often to the end of fleecing guests or gulling husbands. Domestic interiors become tools for managing personal advancement and as such they carry on the negotiation of public concerns around status.

Although the exceptional, separable nature of domestic space is denied in city comedies, a great deal of detail is given about household matter in these plays. Such detail evokes interiors by the naming of representative items. In 2i *A Mad World, My Masters*, Sir Bounteous Progress, a man whose generous hospitality is constantly mocked, discusses the imminent arrival of a Lord Owemuch, actually his nephew Follywit in disguise. The scene's interior nature has already been established by the exit of two knights through one of the doors at the back of the stage, thanking their host for his generosity, and the instant arrival of Owemuch's footman at the other "in haste"(Middleton 1995).

Bounteous fires a series of questions at the footman about his master's description of the house to which he was headed, to see whether it was indeed his own: "Did he name the house with the great turret a'th' top?"(29–30); "Did he speak of a cloth o' gold chamber?"(32–3); "Was there no talk of a fair pair of organs, a great gilt candlestick, and a pair of silver snuffers?"(3–8); "Was there no speech of a long dining room, a huge kitchen, large meat, and a broad dresser board?"(43–4).

When Owemuch is safely installed, Bounteous again plays out his domestic plenty in the linguistic detail of false modesty:

> [...] and now I am as like to bring your lordship to as mean a lodging—a hard down bed i'faith, my lord, poor cambric sheets, and a cloth o'tissue canopy. The curtains indeed were wrought in Venice with the story of the prodigal child in silk and gold; only the swine are left out, my lord, for spoiling the curtains. (2ii, 2–7)

The comedy comes from the social precision of such speeches, but also from the interplay between the presence of bounty in both the audience's and the *characters'* imagination: the way the descriptions provoke a detailed imagination of the objects aids the characters' almost tangible dreams of future plenty, but also stresses its eternally contested physical ownership in the present of the play's representation.

DOMESTIC TRAGEDY

Domestic tragedies, on the other hand, have to be formed from causal narrative stories rather than such satirical set pieces. The events on which they focus occur because of the intricate causalities of individual identities, actions and circumstances. They were often based on stories which had captured the public imagination because of the shocking nature of the crimes they portrayed, crimes in which those crucial power relations of the household were undermined. For instance, *The lamentable and true tragedie of M. Arden of Feversham in Kent, who was most wickedlye murdred, by the meanes of his disloyall and wanton wife, who for the loue she bare to one Mosbie, hyred two desperate ruffins Blackwill and Shakbag, to kill him. Wherin is shewed the great malice and discimulation of a wicked woman, the unsatiable desire of filthie lust and the shamefull end of all murderers* (Wine 1973). The fact that these events had really taken place gave them a particular frisson of dangerous excitement, and their representation must have provoked a different kind of imagination in their audiences, of the socially-specific kind of household spaces likely to be inhabited by such people.

Specific social environments generate action in these plays, and they use the particularities of domestic life to investigate their protagonists' psychology through the connection between objects, spaces and the intensity of emotion. They use, in other words, essentially the same theatrical methods for representing domestic interiors as city comedies, but those dramaturgies are altered by the painfully personal specificity which they take on. When John Frankford banishes his wife for adultery in *A Woman Killed with Kindness*, he articulates their separation through the material qualities of their household: "Choose thee a bed and hangings for a chamber; Take with thee everything that hath thy mark"(xiii, 163–4). Goods are introduced into the narrative as possessions with unique meanings, not as commodities ripe for exchange. Because they are actually used to compose the rooms of a household on stage, as well as the representation of household *plenty*, their material presence is governed by the affective qualities of domestic space. Domestic space, as a location, is crucial to the sense these plays develop of the pressures of environment.

Unlike the majority of early modern plays, domestic tragedies offer a firmly focused perspective, from within the house looking out. Their domestic representation is sustained, and the contrasts which they offer are those between different rooms, or between the domestic and the street outside. The boundedness of domestic space is crucial to their power, and they often focus on the doors at the rear of the stage as a way of drawing attention to the extent to which it is possible to maintain the barrier between inside and outside. In his friend Franklin's house, the soon-to-be-murdered Arden of Faversham's servant agrees to leave the doors unlocked for the assassins. The audience see Arden giving himself an unwitting reprieve by trying these doors from the inside, and then, when they have been re-locked, the assassins try the same doors in the next scene—now representing the outside of the house. Characters publicly assess their motives for such actions. Loyalty, which should tie those within the house to one another and keep others on the outside, is a subject of intense interest—the extent to which the domestic and the non-domestic have clearly differentiated modes of interaction is interrogated.

Within the house, in these plays too, large stage properties are used to construct a sense of different rooms. Conventional scenes such as Anne Frankford's deathbed in Heywood's play, on which she spells out the significance of her husband's decision to "kill her with kindness," are once more centered on one crucial prop. Here, however, the intention is to display the didactic message, and Anne's moralized body itself becomes the focus of attention, rather than the social meanings produced by Allwit's description of his "Fair needlework stools"(3ii, 207) in the christening scene mentioned above. The domestic object provides a meaningful ground for action, representing Anne's resumption of her domestic roles.

Objects in general are particularly significant in these plays, where they appear physically as props rather than being described rhetorically, and are used in some numbers to build up a sense of domestic space. Arden's death is made all the more shocking by its location in his parlor, amongst the table, stools and chair which have been provided for the guests whom he has invited for dinner. And the properties associated with dining are particularly prevalent. Scene VIII of *A Woman Killed With Kindness*, for instance, begins with the stage direction, *Enter 3 or 4 Servingmen, one with a voider and a wooden knife to take away all, another the salt and bread, another the tablecloth and napkins, another the carpet. Jenkin with two lights after them.* The insistence with which such displays of domestic plenty foreground the provision of hospitality is ironically undercut by the less-than-hospitable murders and sexual encounters with which guests and subordinates reward their hosts. It is a characteristic of these plays that the scenes in which domestic life is particularly insistently presented are those in which its meanings are threatened, and the fullness of representation comments ironically on the way actions undercut the careful hierarchies of the household. The domestic interior is the ground for these tragedies, and the idea of the household as a little commonwealth is their subject. That consonance of setting and subject makes for a very intense drama.

There are substantial differences between the operation of domestic interiors in these two genres, then. Some of those differences are particular to the distance which satire establishes between audience and representation, offering, as city comedy's first commentator Brian Gibbons put it, "astringent critical discrimination and the pleasures of glee, disgust, intellectual exercise of wit, rather than sympathetic identification with character, scene and experience"(Gibbons 1980: 6). The kind of imaginative enterprise in which the audience is involved is correspondingly different: an objectifying, evaluating exercise rather than a real engagement with what it might be like to "be there."

But both genres are interested in particularity, indeed they rely upon it. In satire the domestic is marginalized to a role in epitomizing behavior. In domestic tragedy, in which situation is seen to generate action, the material qualities of the household become much more central, and they bear a greater weight of the meaning of the play. City comedy offers a *social* particularity: the pretension-puncturing satire of social foibles and indicative, exaggerated behavior; domestic tragedy offers *personal* particularity, a consideration of the extent to which domestic practice and household space generate tragedy, and how individuals' very distinctive actions lead to adultery and/or murder.

In the tragedies, objects and settings become more realistic the more specific they are to a particular household: they function *more* symbolically, ringing out from the narrative of the play, catching up its emotional complexities and offering themselves for comparison to objects outside the theatre—in *your* home perhaps? Gibbons' assessment of city comedy's mode of representation is equal and opposite: "It is a kind of paradox," he said, "that the more a playwright stylises character and setting [...] stressing underlying patterns in the seemingly contingent circumstances of everyday city life, the more closely he is likely to engage contemporary issues"(Gibbons 1980: 118). The more condensed individuality is into the stylization of telling details, the more it brings issues outside the performance into play, but those issues address social status, not domestic life. Household tragedy and satiric comedy, then, appear to develop different kinds of symbolic mimesis around their employment of domestic objects and interiors, the former personally specific, the latter socially precise. As the meeting point of personal choice and the wider communal meanings of status, the domestic interior has this potential for flexible representation on the bare stages of the pre-Restoration theatre.

NOTES
1. See Foakes, 2001, p. 21; Gurr, 2004a, Chapter 2. Although the Globe did have the greatest capacity, and even the extended Rose Theatre probably only held 2,200 spectators.
2. For analysis of the role of props in this theatre see Harris and Korda (eds), 2002.
3. All quotations are from Wells and Taylor (eds), 1986.

REFERENCES
Anon. 1570. *Homilie Agaynst Disobedience and Wylful Rebellion*. London: Richarde Iugge and Iohn Cawood.

Dessen, Alan. 1984. *Elizabethan Stage Conventions and Modern Interpreters*. Cambridge: Cambridge University Press.

Jonson, Ben 2003. *Epicene*, Edited by Richard Dutton. Manchester: Manchester University Press.

Foakes, R.A. 2001. "Shakespeare's Elizabethan stages." In Russell Jackson and Jonathan Bate (eds), *The Illustrated History of Shakespeare on Stage*, pp. 10–22.

Gibbons, Brian. 1980. *Jacobean City Comedy*, 2nd edn. London: Methuen.

Gouge, William. 1622. *Of Domestical Duties*. London: Printed by Iohn Haviland for William Bladen.

Gurr, Andrew. 2004a. *Playgoing in Shakespeare's London*, 3rd edn. Cambridge: Cambridge University Press.

———. 2004b. "'Within the compass of the city walls': Allegiances in plays for and about the city." In Dieter Mehl, Angela Stock and Anne-Julia Zwierlein (eds) *Plotting Early Modern London: New Essays on Jacobean City Comedy*, pp. 109–122.

Harris, Jonathan Gil and Natasha Korda (eds). 2002. *Staged Properties in Early Modern English Drama*. Cambridge: Cambridge University Press.

Jackson, Russell. 2001. "Actor-managers and the spectacular." In Russell Jackson and Jonathan Bate (eds) *The Illustrated History of Shakespeare on Stage*. Oxford: Oxford University Press, pp. 122–127.

Jackson, Russell and Jonathan Bate (eds). 2001. *The Illustrated History of Shakespeare on Stage*. Oxford: Oxford University Press.

Mehl, Dieter, Angela Stock and Anne-Julia Zwierlein (eds). 2004. *Plotting Early Modern London: New Essays on Jacobean City Comedy*. Aldershot, Hants: Ashgate.

Middleton, Thomas. 1979. *A Critical Edition of Thomas Middleton's Your Five Gallants*. Edited by Clare Lee Colegrove. New York: Garland Pub.

——. 1988. *Five Plays*. Edited by Brian Loughrey and Neil Taylor. Harmondsworth: Penguin.

——. 1995. *A Mad World, My Masters and Other Plays*. Edited by Michael Taylor, Oxford: Oxford University Press.

Streitberger, W.R. (ed.). 1986. *Jacobean and Caroline Revels Accounts, 1603–1642*. Malone Society Collections Volume XIII. Oxford: Oxford University Press for the Malone Society.

Wells, Stanley and Gary Taylor (eds). 1986. *The Oxford Shakespeare*. Oxford: Oxford University Press.

Wine, M.L. 1973. *The Tragedy of Master Arden of Faversham*. London: Methuen.

CHARLES RICE
EVIDENCE, EXPERIENCE AND CONJECTURE: READING THE INTERIOR THROUGH BENJAMIN AND BLOCH

CHARLES RICE IS A LECTURER IN ARCHITECTURE AT THE UNIVERSITY OF NEW SOUTH WALES, SYDNEY, AUSTRALIA. HE HAS ALSO TAUGHT IN HISTORIES AND THEORIES AT THE ARCHITECTURAL ASSOCIATION SCHOOL OF ARCHITECTURE, LONDON. HE IS AUTHOR OF *INHABITING THE DOUBLED INTERIOR: ARCHITECTURE AND BOURGEOIS DOMESTICITY*, WHICH IS FORTHCOMING FROM ROUTLEDGE.

This article looks at the resonances between Walter Benjamin's writing on the bourgeois domestic interior, and Ernst Bloch's investigation of the detective novel. These resonances hinge on the evidence that the interior registers through traces, and how these traces relate to the conjectural knowledge of detection. Explored via Carlo Ginzburg, conjectural knowledge raises the question of experience in modernity, a question crucial to understanding the role of literary narrative in the nineteenth century, as well as the historical emergence of the bourgeois domestic interior at this time.

Ever since the time of Louis Philippe, the bourgeois has shown a tendency to compensate for the absence of any trace of private life in the big city. He tries to do this within the four walls of his apartment. It is as if he made it a point of honor not to allow the traces of his everyday objects and accessories to get lost. Indefatigably, he takes the impression of a host of objects; for his slippers and his watches, his blankets and his umbrellas, he devises coverlets and cases. He has a marked preference for velour and plush, which preserve the imprint of all contact. In the style characteristic of the second empire, the apartment becomes a sort of cockpit. The traces of its inhabitant are molded into the interior. Here is the origin of the detective story, which inquires into these traces and follows these tracks.

Benjamin 1999a: 20

> With these lines, Walter Benjamin gives us a distilled account of the inhabitation of the bourgeois domestic interior. This interior is produced through an infolding, which Benjamin encourages us to consider literally in terms of the interior as a soft and impressionable surface. This surface does not produce a hermetic seal against the external world, but rather is activated through the inhabitant's relation to the city and its world of publicness, business and commerce, and enables a subjectivity and a social identity marked bourgeois to be supported artifactually. The impressionable surface holds onto the artifacts "liberated" from the world of commodities and interiorized for the securing of a private life. The surface folds to encase the inhabitant and these collected objects. The indefatigable collector understands that such a fabrication of the interior is a continual process, a set of techniques and practices that ensures the ongoing viability of a self. Yet the traces registered on the interior's impressionable surface also position the inhabiting subject in a constricting sense. Such traces imply detection, and the detective inevitably begins an investigation at the discovery of a dead body.

In an earlier fragment from *One-Way Street* entitled "Manorially Furnished Ten-Room Apartment," Benjamin describes more fully the relationship between detection and the interior. As Tom Gunning suggests, Benjamin "presents the detective story as a critique of the *intérieur*" (Gunning 2003: 113):

The furniture style of the second half of the nineteenth century has received its only adequate description, and analysis, in a certain type of detective novel at the dynamic centre of which stands the horror of apartments. The arrangement of the furniture is at the same time the site plan of deadly traps, and the suite of rooms prescribes the path of fleeing victims. [...] The bourgeois interior of the 1860s to the 1890s—with its gigantic sideboards distended with carvings, the sunless corners where potted palms sit, the balcony embattled behind its balustrade—fittingly houses only the corpse. "On this sofa the aunt cannot but be murdered." The soulless luxury of furnishings becomes true comfort only in the presence of a dead body. [...] This character of the bourgeois apartment, tremulously awaiting the nameless murderer like a lascivious old lady her gallant, has been penetrated by a number of authors who, as writers of "detective stories"—and perhaps also because in their works part of the bourgeois pandemonium is exhibited—have been denied the reputation they deserve. (Benjamin 1996: 446–447)

The detective novel, and the process of detection that it narrates, exposes the interior, and the "bourgeois pandemonium" at its heart. This exposure, and the concomitant denial of the value of the detective genre as a kind of revenge for this betrayal of the private, has a curious, alternate effect to do with the ordinary, domestic pleasure taken in the genre. Ernst Bloch opens his philosophical view of the detective novel by trying to work out why one might find things as superficial as detective novels enticing:

The setting in which detective stories are enjoyed the most is just too cozy. In a comfortable chair, under the nocturnal floor lamp with tea, rum, and tobacco, personally secure and peacefully immersed in dangerous things, which are shallow. (Bloch 1988: 245)

He discovers—for his philosophical view is in fact a detective investigation—that the enticement is as much about the situation of reading as the material read. The "too cozy" aspect of the interior is precisely what enables the "dangerous things" to entice. Bloch intends the same effect from his own investigation, which he describes as being like "random hunting expeditions [that] flush out game which methodological philosophy can use in its neatly ordered household" (Bloch 1988: 246). The status of what is flushed out is disturbing to such a household. "Something is uncanny—that is how it begins" (Bloch 1988: 245), how both the detective novel begins, and the investigation of its genre.

The uncanny reveals the interior's doubleness. As I have argued elsewhere, the bourgeois domestic interior emerged from the beginning of the nineteenth century as both a representational and a spatial condition, producing a heightened relation to the world of material things, but where this relation took on the flavor of an increasingly de-realized experience (Rice 2004). With reference to

Bloch's cozy situation of reading, the doubled interior is figured precisely in the uncanny slippage between narrative representation, with the imaginative flights it implies, and the spatialization of possible threat as all too real.

I have used this account of the emergence of the doubled interior to critique the conventional methods through which histories of privacy, domesticity and the interior have been written. The problem with these methods stems from the way in which representational evidence of the interior is often read transparently to reconstruct "ways of living in times past." These ways are often seen as part of a developmental trajectory, explaining "where we are today." This sort of thinking tends also to be coupled with a perspective that essentializes the interior as a timeless, universal context for the domestic. For example, a series of studies on the representation of housework in Victorian England has been framed by Vanessa Dickerson in an appeal to the essential:

> House and home are part of an ongoing natural phenomenon: all animals have habitats. The houses in which human beings dwell, however, accrue so much more significance when one acknowledges how "divisions of space and social formations are intimately associated." (Dickerson 1996: xiii)

There is an attempt here to mark out a difference for the "human habitat," but one that seems to be subject to the forces of progressive evolution. Benjamin recognized the problem to do with this view of the domestic:

> The difficulty in reflecting on dwelling: on the one hand, there is something age-old—perhaps eternal—to be recognized here, the image of that abode of the human being in the maternal womb; on the other hand, this motif of primal history notwithstanding, we must understand dwelling in its most extreme form as a condition of nineteenth-century existence. (Benjamin 1999a: 220)

The extreme form of dwelling in the nineteenth century was the bourgeois domestic interior. In his exposés for *The Arcades Project*, Benjamin outlined the historical emergence, consolidation, and ultimate liquidation of the interior within the span of the nineteenth century. His own temporal location in interwar Europe necessitated an anti-nostalgic view of the domestic, prey as it was to the essentializing and mythologizing thinking of a regressive politics.

In this article I want to extend this anti-essentialist line of thinking to develop further an account of the evidence of the interior, and methods for reading that evidence, that seek to figure its fragmentary, occluded, and ultimately "archaic" sense, a sense that preserves the doubleness of its historical emergence. I shall follow up on Benjamin's suggestion that the bourgeois domestic interior was the site for the birth of the detective genre by tracing the ways it resonates with Bloch's argument for the genre providing both a method of detection, and a focus on the interior as the most intense site of detection. This line of thinking asks: how does the bourgeois interior surface in literature, especially in a genre of writing that might be discredited as literature? Thinking about the surfacing of the interior in this way is akin to thinking about the very spatial logic of the interior as a surfacing of the inside space of architecture, as a transformation of the "respectable house" of architecture into the space of commercialized decoration. This mode of thinking through—indeed, investigating—opens the interior to a mode of knowledge that is conjectural.

CONJECTURE, EXPERIENCE AND THE BIRTH OF NARRATIVE

Carlo Ginzburg has argued that an epistemological paradigm which may be described as conjectural or evidential emerged in a particular way towards the end of the nineteenth century, becoming "very much operative in spite of never having become explicit theory" (Ginzburg 1986: 96). This paradigm belongs to the detective, but has as its most crucial figure the art historian Giovanni Morelli who, in the late nineteenth century, revolutionized the method for the attribution of old master paintings by paying attention to the particular rendering of what had been considered insignificant details, such as ears and fingernails. These details seemed to fall outside the realm of conscious technique, but as such revealed the most "personal" imprint of a particular artist's hand. Morelli's method is Holmesian, or, rather, as Ginzburg suggests, Sherlock Holmes "discovers the perpetrator of a crime [...] on the basis of evidence imperceptible to most people. [...] Sherlock Holmes literally 'morellizes'" (Ginzburg 1986: 97–98). And in a doubling of the method about which he writes, Ginzburg traces Morelli's direct influence on Freud's thinking and method, characterizing it thus: "our inadvertent little gestures reveal our character far more authentically than any formal posture that we may carefully prepare" (Wind 1985: 38, quoted in Ginzburg 1986: 98). The reading of pictorial marks (Morelli), the detecting of clues (Holmes) and the analysis of symptoms (Freud) carve out a mode of knowing that is conjectural. Ginzburg argues that such a mode found its "implicit justification in the denial that reality is transparent" (Ginzburg 1986: 105).

Stemming from this initial tracing, Ginzburg has a larger claim to make about conjecture that is useful in thinking about the evidence of the interior: that narrative is founded within this conjectural paradigm. While claiming the modernity of such a paradigm, Ginzburg argues that its roots are ancient, even mythical (Ginzburg 1986: 116). He writes of an "oriental fable" in which three brothers come across a man who has lost a camel. Though they have not seen the animal (which in variants of the fable is a horse or a donkey) the men are able to describe exactly its particular traits by reading the marks it made along a track. This ability leads to their arrest for its theft. Ginzburg remarks:

> Obviously, the three brothers are repositories of some sort of venatic lore, even if they are not necessarily hunters. This knowledge is characterized by the ability to construct from apparently insignificant experimental data a complex reality that could not be experienced directly. Also, the data is always arranged by the observer in such a way as to produce a narrative sequence, which could be expressed most simply as 'someone passed this way'. Perhaps the actual idea of narration (as distinct from charms, exorcisms or invocation) may have originated in a hunting society, relating the experience of deciphering tracks. [...] The hunter would have been the first 'to tell a story' because he alone was able to read, in the silent, nearly imperceptible tracks left by his prey, a coherent sequence of events. (Ginzburg 1986: 103)

The mythological dimension of this founding of narrative is important to consider in terms of the way in which it was taken up in Voltaire's *Zadig*, the protagonist making the same sort of "diagnosis" of two animals from their tracks in the sand (Voltaire 1990: 130–134). Ginzburg writes how what came to be known by the late nineteenth century as "Zadig's method" directly influenced Poe and Conan Doyle, as well as emerging sciences including paleontology, which would come under the designation of "divination directed toward the past" (Ginzburg 1986: 117).

In a wider sense, the link between narration and conjectural knowledge relates to the status in the nineteenth century of long experience (*Erfahrung*), the sort of experience implied in the conjectural skill of the three brothers/Zadig, and passed down via the oral tradition of the story. Ginzburg writes:

> For an increasingly large number of readers, access to specific experiences was mediated by means of the printed page. The novel actually provided the bourgeoisie with both a substitute for and reformulation of initiation rites—that is, for access to experience in general. (Ginzburg 1986: 115)

Yet for Benjamin, the rise of the novel as substitute is evidence itself for the atrophying of long experience: "The birthplace of the novel is the individual in his isolation, the individual who can no longer speak of his concerns in exemplary fashion, who himself lacks counsel and can give none" (Benjamin 2002: 146). As Martin Jay suggests a propos Benjamin's argument:

> the experience [novels] depict is thus that of *Erlebnis* [momentary experience] at its emptiest. The fate of the characters, indeed their very deaths, can only provide a simulacrum of meaning for readers, whose lives are deprived of it. (Jay 1998: 53)

In Benjamin's thinking, there is a difference between the story and the novel, and the interior becomes bound up in this difference. In his essay "Experience and Poverty," Benjamin writes:

> Everyone knew precisely what experience [*Erfahrung*] was: older people had always passed it on to younger ones. It was handed down in short form to sons and grandsons, with the authority of age, in proverbs; with an often long-winded eloquence, as tales, sometimes as stories from foreign lands, at the fireside. (Benjamin 1999b: 731)

The bourgeois domestic interior emerges in this kind of appeal to the "fireside," but, along with the novel, as a kind of compensation for the very impossibility of the story, and the sense of experience it transmits. It emerges to support its inhabitant "in his illusions" (Benjamin 1999a: 19), creating the semblance of long experience through the techniques and practices of securing a private life.

In relation to this interior, the detective novel is neither the story nor the novel proper, and this might be another way of explaining why it is held in disrepute. It begins at the point at which the novel would end, with the death of the one who would otherwise have been its protagonist. This point of beginning is the dissolution of a life story, and, as such, is beyond the way in which experience might be redeemed, in however illusory a way, in narrative form. Instead, the remnants of experience become available to a narrative that is conjectural—and that echoes the "birth" of narrative—but that is conjectural precisely about the scattered remnants found after the event of the shattering of long experience. Objects that once held meaning for the inhabitant now hold a different significance for the detective who inspects the traces they have left. The interior formed to capture such traces, an interior that liberated the inhabitant into an illusory but expansive world of experience, now reveals the posthumous inhabitant before an external, analytical gaze.

DETECTION AND THE OMITTED BEGINNING

The event which launches the detective novel, the emblematic "death of the inhabitant," is not, however, able to be captured within its schema. As Bloch suggests: "The problem of the omitted beginning affects the entire detective genre, gives it its form: the form of a picture puzzle, the hidden part of which predates the picture and only gradually enters into it" (Bloch 1988: 264). The omitted beginning is precisely that event which removes the figure who could have become the protagonist of a long experience, however illusory. The detective steps into the frame in place of this missing protagonist, at the point only the traces of this protagonist's removal, and the concomitant shattering of experience, are left. This event, which Bloch also terms "the un-narrated factor" (Bloch 1988: 255), is a "misdeed that is conveniently home-delivered," but one that "shuns the light of day and lingers in the background of the story. It must be brought to light and this process itself is the exclusive theme" (Bloch 1988: 249). Thus what attempts to be shown in the detective novel is unrepresentable. It always stands outside the story, and as such drives the logic of a detective reconstruction. What is uncovered and pieced together is evidence that can only indicate in an obscure fashion this un-narrated factor, this omitted beginning. Evidence is not self-evidence: "detective expeditions [...] search, observe, and follow nothing but clues along the way. Indeed, all they are is a hunt for sufficient evidence in narrative form" (Bloch 1988: 246).

The home-delivered aspect of the un-narrated factor relates precisely to what the interior (as home) conceals within itself. Referencing Benjamin directly, Bloch writes about the decorum that interior decoration is meant to maintain actually creating an "inauthentic environment" (Bloch 1988: 252), one full of duplicity: "the ultimate clue in a detective novel can and usually will consist in the unmasking of the most unexpected, least suspected person as the perpetrator" (Bloch 1988: 253). The un-narrated factor is ultimately oedipal for Bloch in a quite literal sense: "a veiled misdeed precedes the creation of the *world itself*" (Bloch 1988: 258). This leads Bloch to the heart of the Freudian method: "The conviction that the more neatly the mask conceals, the less salutary that which goes on behind it, gives rise to a deep suspicion of draperies and facades directed at all that ideal and upright superficiality that is too beautiful or too comfortable to be true" (Bloch 1988: 254). Benjamin himself casts this sort of thinking in terms of the materiality of the interior, bringing to bear a perspective which Bloch terms "micrological" (Bloch 1988: 251), and reinforcing the idea that evidence presents itself as a picture puzzle:

> The importance of movable property, as compared with immovable property. Here our task is slightly easier. Easier to blaze a way to the heart of things abolished or superseded, in order to decipher the contours of the banal as picture puzzle. (Benjamin 1999a: 212)

The more this deciphering becomes about material evidence, the more it links to the specific operations of dream interpretation. In his own words, Freud presents us with a way of understanding what is at stake in the picture puzzles that Benjamin and Bloch recognize as features of both interior and detective novel:

> a dream is a conglomerate which, for the purposes of investigation, must be broken up once more into fragments. On the other hand, however, it will be observed that a psychical force is at work in dreams which creates this apparent connectedness, which, that is to say, submits this material produced by the dream-work to a "secondary revision." (Freud 1953: 449)

The bourgeois domestic interior is dreamlike in this complex way. In order to investigate the interior, its wholeness, its "apparent connectedness" must be broken up. Its evidence must be treated as a picture puzzle; the fragmented dream content must be explained with reference to particular details that have their significance apart from their manifest appearance, but nonetheless provide access to the "un-narrated factor," that which lies veiled behind the appearances of the dream. But the interior is itself a space for the knitting together of disparate elements in a kind of secondary revision that maintains the semblance of continuity and wholeness, the semblance of long experience.

For its part, the detective novel lays out this analysis, and hence participates in the picture-puzzle quality of the dream. It too presents a coherent narrative as an explanation of what remains beyond representation in that narrative. But the detective narrative is not simply co-incident with the interior. Their difference, the status of one as an analysis of the other, can be designated with a temporal division. The detective novel comes after the "event" that dissolves the coherence of the interior into the picture puzzle of its fragments. It figures the time of the interior as prehistorical, and in this way the detective's micrological gaze might be cast as paleontological, to use Ginzburg's terminology. In this way we are reminded of Benjamin's *Arcades Project* as an archaeology of nineteenth-century Paris, one that is intimately tied to concepts of the dream and of awakening. Elsewhere I have argued that the bourgeois domestic interior gives *The Arcades Project* an organization that escapes a determined structure, and therefore the charge that it remained fragmentary because unfinished. Rather, the bourgeois domestic interior bequeathed to it an organization that meant that the fragmentary material collected could remain provisional in time and space, allowing for an active sifting and piecing together of evidence (Rice 2005). Benjamin's own description of his technique of assembly in *The Arcades Project* communicates this interiorized construction:

> Method of this project: literary montage. I needn't say anything. Merely show. I shall purloin no valuables, appropriate no

ingenious formulations. But the rags, the refuse—these I will not inventory but allow, in the only way possible, to come into their own: by making use of them. (Benjamin 1999a: 460)

We might immediately compare this description of method with Bloch's description of the colportage aspect of the detective novel:

the detective novel, especially the average variety, has the advantage of partaking of the peculiar form of 'colportage', a form that consistently preserves significations long excluded from 'better' literature, and that is not to be equated with kitsch or trash. [...] To sum up: colportage contains significations which in part are also present in the loftier realms of poetry and philosophy; however, they are seldom so disconnected and haphazard there. (Bloch 1988: 249)

What I shall emphasize in this comparison is the way in which a fragmentary organization gives us a clue for understanding how dream and awakening bind the interior and the detective novel together.

THE EMERGING PICTURE OF THE INTERIOR

The provisional, interiorized organization of *The Arcades Project* allows for knowledge to be formed in "lightning flashes" (Benjamin 1999a: 456) which are registered in a "present" of interpretation. These flashes illuminate an image whose sense is formed in this emerging, momentary way. This image carries the sense of the hidden, that element which founds the event of detection, but forever stands outside of the unfolding time of the detection. This sense of an illuminated (dialectical) image enables knowledge to work in a particular way:

What distinguishes images from the "essences" of phenomenology is their historical index. [...] These images are to be thought of entirely apart from the categories of the "human sciences," from so-called habitus, from style, and the like. For the historical index of the images not only says that they belong to a particular time; it says, above all, that they attain legibility only at a particular time. And indeed, this acceding "to legibility" constitutes a specific critical point in the movement at their interior. (Benjamin 1999a: 462–463)

If we take the interior as a specific sort of image—in this way highlighting the representational sense of its doubleness—its acceding to legibility takes place within the construction of the detective narrative. Thus the interior surfaces in literature. It does not exist outside of such moments of emergence or surfacing, except as the archaic, scattered remnants of an event whose temporality is irreconcilable with the time of a developmental narrative. This surfacing of the interior in literature is also the point of its expiration, the "closing of its case." The moments when Benjamin was at his most pragmatic with respect to the political realities that he faced can be found in his thoughts on the simultaneous illumination and liquidation of the bourgeois domestic interior. For Benjamin, this interior can be seen in its precise historical contours at the exact moment that it is superseded by a culture of transparency. It is rendered in *The Arcades Project* with such an immersive, dreamlike consistency, a consistency of both form and content, in order to induce an awakening from it, and from the dangerous hold it had over the complacent culture of Benjamin's time:

> If you enter a bourgeois room of the 1880s, for all the coziness it radiates, the strongest impression you receive may well be, "You've got no business here". And in fact you have no business in that room, for there is no spot on which the owner has not left his mark—the ornaments on the mantelpiece, the antimacassars on the armchairs, the transparencies in the windows, the screen in front of the fire. A neat phrase by Brecht helps us out here: "Erase the traces!" is the refrain in the first poem of his *Lesebuch für Städtebewohner* [*Reader for City-Dwellers*]. [...] This has now been achieved by Scheerbart, with his glass, and the Bauhaus, with its steel. They have created rooms in which it is hard to leave traces. "It follows form the foregoing," Scheerbart declared a good twenty years ago, "that we can surely talk about a 'culture of glass.' The new glass-milieu will transform humanity utterly. And now it remains only to be wished that the new glass-culture will not encounter too many enemies." (Benjamin 1999b: 734)

Erasing the traces might mean obliterating the mode of the detective. The transparency promised in modernism would put paid to the possibility of an "un-narrated factor" that could be found in and also be concealed by the duplicity of the bourgeois domestic interior. Yet at the end, even in this utopian promise of a transparent domesticity, we find a kind of meta-surveillance at play, and here the uncanny re-emerges. Here is Benjamin recounting part of his experience of a visit to Moscow in 1926–27:

> In Moscow I lived in a hotel in which almost all the rooms were occupied by Tibetan lamas who had come to Moscow for a congress of Buddhist churches. I was struck by the number of doors in the corridors that were always left ajar. What had at first seemed accidental began to be disturbing. I found out that in these rooms lived members of a sect who had sworn never to occupy closed rooms. [...] To live in a glass house is a

revolutionary virtue par excellence. It is also an intoxication, a moral exhibitionism, that we badly need. Discretion concerning one's own existence, once an aristocratic value, has become more and more an affair of petty-bourgeois parvenus. (Benjamin 1999c: 209)

In this unsettling domestic, detection is the pre-existing condition. The relation between detection and the interior has been reversed, or, rather, after the erasure of the interior consequent upon the erasure of traces, all that is left is a kind of pure detective vision upon which to found a new, "post-interior" domesticity. Yet rather than there truly being an erasure of traces, the material change in the surfaces of the domestic—from the velvet and plush of the bourgeois interior to the glass surfaces of modernism—indicates a shift in the control over the registering of traces. Where the trace had once been the province of the inhabitant, and had been used as a way of securing a private life away from the alienating forces of the metropolis, it now aligned more strongly with an administrative and governmental apparatus directed towards keeping a notionally "public" record. This is the point at which the individual detective's conjectural skill is folded into the emerging metropolitan police force, and the systematization of evidence against a mechanized apparatus of criminal detection (Gunning 1995; Ginzburg 1986: 118–125).

While the detective may have arrived on the scene after the demise of the private bourgeois individual, and stepped in for this protagonist after the demise of the novelistic narrative of self-formation, the detective's own sense of long experience, an ability in conjuring up the image of an event not witnessed but only traced, is eclipsed by the growth of an apparatus of detection increasingly reliant on the automatic registering of traces. The trace left against velvet transmutes to the trace left against the photographic plate (Benjamin 1999d: 527). Once again, the domestic enticements of the detective genre are precisely those that surround its loss. These are enticements that are found when such an individual figure as the detective slips quietly into myth, and they are found in interiors whose too-coziness equates to a mythic conception of the bourgeois domestic interior.

REFERENCES

Benjamin, Walter. 1996. "One-Way Street." In Marcus Bullock and Michael W. Jennings (eds) *Selected Writings Volume 1: 1913–1926*, pp. 444–488. Cambridge, MA and London: The Belknap Press of Harvard University Press.

———. 1999a. *The Arcades Project*. Edited by Rolf Tiedemann. Cambridge, MA and London: The Belknap Press of Harvard University Press.

———. 1999b. "Experience and Poverty." In Marcus Bullock, Howard Eiland and Gary Smith (eds) *Selected Writings Volume 2: 1927–1934*, pp. 731–736. Cambridge, MA and London: The Belknap Press of Harvard University Press.

———. 1999c. "Surrealism: The Last Snapshot of the European Intelligensia." In Marcus Bullock, Howard Eiland and Gary Smith (eds) *Selected Writings Volume 2: 1927–1934*, pp. 207–221. Cambridge, MA and London: The Belknap Press of Harvard University Press.

———. 1999d. "Little History of Photography." In Marcus Bullock, Howard Eiland and Gary Smith (eds) *Selected Writings Volume 2: 1927–1934*, pp. 507–530. Cambridge, MA and London: The Belknap Press of Harvard University Press.

———. 2002. "The Storyteller: Observations on the Work of Nikolai Leskov." In Marcus Bullock, Howard Eiland and Gary Smith (eds) *Selected Writings Volume 3: 1935–1938*, pp. 143–166. Cambridge, MA and London: The Belknap Press of Harvard University Press.

Bloch, Ernst. 1988. "A Philosophical View of the Detective Novel." In *The Utopian Function of Art and Literature*, pp. 245–264. Cambridge, MA and London: MIT Press.

Dickerson, Vanessa (ed.). 1996. *Keeping the Victorian House: A Collection of Essays*. New York and London: Garland.

Freud, Sigmund. 1953. "The Interpretation of Dreams." In James Strachey (ed.) *The Standard Edition of the Complete Psychological Works of Sigmund Freud*, vol. V, pp. 339–621. London: The Hogarth Press.

Ginzburg, Carlo. 1986. "Clues: Roots of an Evidential Paradigm." In *Myths, Emblems, Clues*, pp. 96–125. London: Hutchinson Radius.

Gunning, Tom. 1995. "Tracing the Individual Body: Photography, Detectives, and Early Cinema." In Leo Charney and Vanessa R. Schwartz (eds) *Cinema and the Invention of Modern Life*, pp. 15–45. Berkeley and London: University of California Press.

———. 2003. "The Exterior as *Intérieur*: Benjamin's Optical Detective." *boundary 2* 30(1): 105–129.

Jay, Martin. 1998. "Experience Without a Subject: Walter Benjamin and the Novel." In *Cultural Semantics: Keywords of Our Time*, pp. 47–61. London: Athlone.

Rice, Charles. 2004. "Rethinking Histories of the Interior." *The Journal of Architecture* 9(3): 275–287.

———. 2005 (forthcoming). "Walter Benjamin's Interior History." In Andrew Benjamin (ed.) *Walter Benjamin and History*. London: Continuum.

Voltaire. 1990. "Zadig, or Destiny. A Tale of the Orient." In *Candide and Other Stories*, pp. 122–202. Oxford: Oxford University Press.

Wind, Edgar. 1985. *Art and Anarchy*. London: Duckworth.

NICOLA WILSON
REPRODUCING THE HOME IN ROBERT TRESSELL'S *THE RAGGED TROUSERED PHILANTHROPISTS* AND D. H. LAWRENCE'S *SONS AND LOVERS*

AFTER GRADUATING FROM THE UNIVERSITY OF DURHAM IN ENGLISH LITERATURE IN 2001, NICOLA WILSON UNDERTOOK A MASTERS IN WOMEN'S STUDIES AT OXFORD UNIVERSITY FROM 2001–2002. SHE IS CURRENTLY TEACHING AND WORKING ON HER PHD THESIS AT THE UNIVERSITY OF WARWICK, WHICH IS PROVISIONALLY TITLED, "REPRODUCING THE HOME: MOTHERS, MOTHERING AND WORKING-CLASS WRITING IN ENGLAND 1913–68." THIS ARTICLE IS TAKEN FROM THE FIRST CHAPTER.

This paper examines a central concern in the texts of *The Ragged Trousered Philanthropists* (1914) and *Sons and Lovers* (1913)—the figure of the home and the mother within it. Situating the author's preoccupation with the domestic interior alongside contemporary social concerns about the houses of the working-classes and the nature of the familial relations that went on within them, I argue that the ways of seeing into the house in these texts are intimately related to the *place* of the embodied author. Tressell and Lawrence's habitation of the class structure—their lived relation to the places of class—determines their reproduction of the working-class home and accounts for the different ways in which it is used in each of the novels, as symbol of the body politic and site of psychological longings respectively.

> Robert Noonan (1870–1911) and David Herbert Lawrence (1885–1930) were associated with many different houses through the course of their turbulent lifetimes. Noonan, pen-name Tressell, was born and brought up in Dublin, and spent time in Cape Town and Johannesburg before moving to Hastings in 1901. Lawrence meanwhile, born in Eastwood in Nottinghamshire, traveled the globe in his thirties and lived most of his life in exile. As any participant in the Hastings "Tressell Trail" or Eastwood's Lawrentian "Blue Line Trail" will note, both men occupied a number of different addresses in the towns which became the inspiration for their imaginative landscapes.

This article considers the authors' preoccupation with the home as a central imaginative device in their first published novels, *The Ragged Trousered Philanthropists* (1914) and *Sons and Lovers* (1913) respectively.[1] Situating the texts' reproduction of the home alongside contemporary social concerns about the houses of the working classes and the nature of the familial relations that went on within them, I argue that it is the figure of the home and the mother (within it) that consumes the attention of the narrative gaze. Bearing in mind that it is with these texts that Tressell and Lawrence came to be read as the "forefathers" of twentieth-century working-class writing in Britain, the article explores how this concern with the house is intimately related to the *place* of the embodied author. The authors' respective habitation of the class structure—their lived relation to the places of class—determines their treatment of the working-class home and interior, and their ways of seeing into it. It is through their treatment, or reproduction, of the house in the texts that the author seeks to work through their understandings of class.

This reading of the authors' reproduction of the home in the novels requires an appreciation of the intimacy between class, place, and the gaze. Raymond Williams and Pierre Bourdieu, among others, have sought to draw attention to the spatial dynamics of class, and not just its economic determinants. According to this view, the possibility of being at home in space is a highly classed act and is inextricably tied up with the way in which one is positioned by others (the way one is looked at). It is a constant refrain of the hands in *The Ragged Trousered Philanthropists*, for instance, that certain places are "not for the likes of us." The distinction made here in the narratives' ways of seeing into the home thus draws upon an understanding of the authors' positioning within the class structure. The more cosmopolitan Tressell, well-traveled and boasting a fair amount of "cultural capital" by the time of writing *The Ragged Trousered Philanthropists*, uses the image of the house as a metaphor for the body politic and to interrogate the workings of a classed society. Though during the period of writing the manuscript, from 1906 to 1910, Tressell was precariously employed as a workman in Hastings, his experience of empire, as well as a respectable upbringing in Ireland, opened up the vantage point available to him as he came to write his "picture of working-class life in a small town in the south of England" (this is how he describes the novel in the preface). The narrative's way of seeing into the individual homes of the philanthropists, sharing something with contemporary philanthropic discourses looking into the houses of the working-classes, demonstrates a concern to chart the exploitation of those at the margins of society and to bring the un-narrated into literary consciousness.

For D. H. Lawrence on the other hand, writing *Sons and Lovers* in his early twenties as a young man looking back on a working-class childhood, the house is treated in a more explicitly psychological way in order to negotiate a class-based "anxiety of origins." This is an anxiety of origins that is distinct from, yet follows in the tradition of, the Bloomsian "anxiety of influence" (Bloom 2000) and Gilbert and Gubar's "anxiety of authorship."(Gilbert & Gubar 1979) Lawrence's experience of place—up until writing the final version of *Sons and Lovers* between July and November 1912 during his elopement to Italy with Frieda Weekley—was much more circumspect in comparison with Tressell's. His reproduction of the house is therefore more closely associated with the longings of childhood.

REPRODUCING THE HOUSE: TRESSELL

> Public conferences and meetings are being held everywhere on the subject, and housing committees formed; statesmen debate the problem; Churches discuss it; co-operative societies and trade unions pass resolutions upon it; and municipal elections ring with the cry for healthier and more wholesome dwellings.
>
> Haw 1900: iv

By the time of the publication of *The Ragged Trousered Philanthropists* and *Sons and Lovers*, the working-class abode was more than a fit object for contemplation; it was constantly being looked at and physically intruded upon. From the seminal impact of Charles Booth and Seebohm Rowntree's research, to a concern about the condition of working-class bodies following on from the poor status of potential recruits to the Boer War, an interlocking set of concerns about the state of the nation, the empire, and poverty meant that the working-class interior was a site for surveillance and discussion.[2] The houses of the working-classes had been the site of philanthropic and utopian urges for much of the nineteenth-century (take for example the created communities of New Lanark, Copley and Saltaire). Yet it was eugenic and nationalistic fears that came to focus a more general concern with working-class living spaces into a discourse preoccupied with interiors in the years immediately prior to 1910. It was no longer sufficient merely to imagine the working-class abode as totality; the intrepid must see inside room by room. As Marion Fitzgerald was to advise in her lecture to health visitors, "How to Visit in the Homes," the negotiation of the working-class interior was crucial:

> Do not pay "door-step" visits, you must succeed in getting invited into the family living room. [...] You may find, in spite of the mother's satisfaction, a miserable little wisp of humanity. (Fitzgerald 1915: 38–40)

As Fitzgerald's remarks here suggest, if the working-class home was a site for surveillance during this period, it was the woman inside the home (and in particular the mother) who was the final resting place for the outside visitors' gaze and instruction. With the realization that, "we cannot get soldiers or men ready-made. We must go back to infancy and motherhood" (Saleeby 1915: 5), fears of a declining birth rate and high figures of infant mortality produced a burgeoning strand of public opinion which focused a concern for the child within the working-class abode through what John Burns, at the first National Conference on Infant Mortality in 1906, described as "good or bad motherhood" (quoted in Pember Reeves 1913: x). In *Maternity: Letters from Working Women*, published in 1915, the Women's Co-Operative Guild politicized their demand for a host of state interventions to improve the care of maternity and infancy through recourse to a wider discourse of empire:

> Action is necessary also because, for the lack of it, the nation is weakened. [...] The ideas for which Britain stands can only prevail so long as they are backed by a sufficient mass of numbers. [...] Under existing conditions we waste, before birth and in infancy, a large part of our possible population. (Llewelyn Davies 1915: xii)

The importance of looking at the working-class mother was dictated by her capacity as child-rearer. In Dr. J.W Ballantyne's *Expectant Motherhood: Its Supervision and Hygiene*, published in 1914 and written for an educated audience of potential mothers, it is concern for the body of the infant that prevails, "we can only reach the unborn infant through the mother who carries him" (Ballantyne 1914: x).

Concern with the houses of the poor during this period thus came to be conflated with the surveillance and monitoring of working-class reproduction.

In *The Ragged Trousered Philanthropists*, Tressell inhabits this concern to examine the working-class interior. The main character, Frank Owen, who can loosely be seen as a mouthpiece for Tressell's politics, is a member of the local Trades Council, the delegates of which pressed for increased house-building in towns throughout the early years of the twentieth century.[3] Owen lives with his wife and son in a home that bears the traces of Tressell's familial abode in Hastings between 1903 and 1906. Though most of the novel was written up later, in a flat in nearby St Leonards, it is the interior of 115 Milward Road that provides the imaginative landscape for Owen's home in the text. The following is taken from Chapter Six:

> Owen and his family occupied the top floor of a house that had once been a large private dwelling but which had been transformed into a series of flats. [...] At one time this had been a most aristocratic locality, but most of the former residents had migrated to the new suburb at the west of the town. [...] Owen's wife and little son were waiting for him in the living room. This room was about twelve feet square and the ceiling—which was low and irregularly shaped, showing in places the formation of the roof—had been decorated by Owen with painted ornaments. [...] Although there was a bright fire, the room was very cold, being so close to the roof. The wind roared loudly round the gables, shaking the house in a way that threatened every moment to hurl it to the ground. (Tressell 1993: 76, 78, 87).

Interior spaces within houses are the most important site of action in the text and the place to which the narrative gaze most often returns. Whilst, as the painters and decorators work a six-and-a-half day week, it is their workplace that is the central structuring interior in the narrative, the reader is also taken in succession into the homes of the four central families (the Eastons, Lindens, Owens and Newmans). The depiction of the first home that the reader looks into, that of the Eastons—the Financiers in Chapter Three—is striking for the level of detail with which the interior is surveyed. As Easton enters the home (his wife Ruth is inside), the narrative gaze observes each of the house's four rooms in turn, noting the objects within minutely. Take for example the following description:

> The front door opened into a passage about two feet six inches wide and ten feet in length, covered with oilcloth. [...] The first door on the left led into the front sitting-room, an apartment about nine feet square, with a bay window. This room was very

rarely used and was always very tidy and clean. The mantelpiece was of wood painted black and ornamented with jagged streaks of red and yellow. [...] There was a small iron fender with fire-irons to match, and on the mantelshelf stood a clock in a polished wood case, a pair of blue glass vases, and some photographs in frames. The floor was covered with oilcloth of a tile pattern in yellow and red. (Tressell 1993: 49)

The voraciousness of the narrative gaze here shares some of the characteristics of revelation—a bringing of the working-class home into consciousness—of contemporary philanthropic documents. Emblematic of such discourse is the Fabian Women's Group's research into the daily lives and budgets of working-class women living in Lambeth, published the year before Tressell's manuscript with the title, *Round about a Pound a Week*. Through recourse to such close observation and measurement, groups such as the Fabian Women were able to show that the working man "pays more per cubic foot of space than the rich man does" (Pember Reeves 1913: 23). For the vast majority of the population before 1914 the possibility of house-ownership was still slim, and the weekly payment of rent was the largest fixed item in the household budget. The novel's detailed way of seeing into the domestic interior is also suggestive of a way of life whereby each object is regarded in light of its potential threat or value. Still scanning the Easton's living quarters, the narrator notes:

Some of these things, as the couch and the chairs, Easton had bought second-hand and had done up himself. The table, oilcloth, fender, hearthrug, etc, had been obtained on the hire system and were not yet paid for. (Tressell 1993: 50)

What is different about Tressell's gaze into the domestic interior, however, is the place of the voyeur. There is a tradition of writing about the working-classes in terms of their habitation of the den, whereby the urban explorer charts the wastes of the city in order to discover the apparently mute under-classes in their seemingly inexplicable surroundings. Even in a sympathetic treatise such as *Round about a Pound a Week*, the journey of the social ethnographer is framed in epic terms. Thus the way into the district is arduous for the women, involving a tram ride from Victoria to Vauxhall, the navigation of Kennington Lane, followed by Vauxhall Walk, Lambeth Walk and The Walk. In *The Ragged Trousered Philanthropists*, this way of seeing into the text—drawing on the trope of the journey across space from clearly defined subject position to incomprehensible site of otherness—belongs to those characters which possess authority. The men painting and decorating "The Cave," the landed house the philanthropists are working on, are increasingly pinioned to the spot (associated firstly with the room they are working in, and then with the particular object they are painting—radiator, window, skirting). It is with their employers that the reader can move across space, taking in the prospect of the house from a longer view:

> Mr Hunter, at the moment the reader first makes his acquaintance [...] was executing a kind of strategical movement in the direction of the house where Crass and his mates were working. He kept to one side of the road because by doing so he could not be perceived by those within the house until the instant of his arrival. When he was within about a hundred yards of the gate he dismounted. (Tressell 1993: 35)

Once over the threshold, the employers command access across the interior of the house whilst the workers increasingly experience place as confinement.

The idea of property as a defining marker of class has been a constant from the early nineteenth century. In 1828, for example, William Mackinnon commented that, "the only means by which the classes of society can be defined, in a community where the laws are equal, is from the amount of property, either real or personal, possessed by individuals" (quoted in Briggs 1983: 15). Yet the house itself, and more particularly its interior, has largely been absent from such commentary. From his opening depiction of "The Cave" however, "it was a large old-fashioned three-storied building standing in about an acre of ground, and situated about a mile outside the town of Mugsborough," Tressell is concerned to rewrite the actuality of the house into ideas about property and class (Tressell 1993: 15). Just as the self-conscious narrator is constantly at pains to draw attention to the labor process behind the work of fiction, so the plot of *The Ragged Trousered Philanthropists* works to deconstruct the notion of the grand old house of fiction as a *fait accompli*. As Ian Haywood observes, "the setting reverses the usual narrative perspective from which large houses are seen in fiction" (Haywood 1997: 30). Newly purchased by Mr. Sweater and being altered and redecorated by Rushton & Co, "The Cave" is a site for oppression and corruption, depravity and, ultimately, terror (one of the characters, Philpot, is killed in an accident whilst painting the gables). During one of his socialist lectures, Owen draws upon the image of the dilapidated landed-house as the ultimate way to describe the current body politic:

> And suppose that the house was badly built, the walls so constructed that they drew and retained moisture, the roof broken and leaky, the drains defective, the doors and windows ill-fitting and the rooms badly shaped and draughty. If you were asked to name, in a word, the cause of the ill-health of the people who lived there you would say—the house. [...] Well,

> we're all of us living in a house called the Money System; and as a result most of us are suffering from a disease called poverty. (Tressell 1993: 147)

The action that takes place within the interior rooms of the house also plays out the workings of the class system. The kitchen is a place for the men: a site for debate, refreshment, dirty stories and community. The drawing-room meanwhile, is where the employers meet to hold forth upon the progress of the house and local politics, and where Owen, as the most skilled artist of the group, is commissioned to paint a Moorish frieze upon the walls (his enthusiasm for this work should be read alongside William Morris's critique of the degradation of craftsmanship in the contemporary workplace). Tressell's use of the image of the house as a central metaphor for the workings of society is one of the many ways in which he is influenced by Dickens' narrative technique.

To argue that the interior of the home is a crucial site of narrative action in *The Ragged Trousered Philanthropists* is to engage with the ways of seeing the women in the text. Tressell's depiction of the women inside the philanthropists' homes (and it is most often women, and children, who occupy this interior space: Ruth Easton, Nora Owen, Mary Linden, Mrs. Newman) points to the complexity of his engagement with contemporary views regarding the gendered occupation of space by the working-class family. Tressell was certainly convinced of the need for a "family wage," which was increasingly a part of trade union strategy from the mid-nineteenth century onwards. Family wage campaigners believed that the solution to child poverty lay in ensuring that the male wage earner had a sufficient income to support all his dependents, without further state intervention. In *The Ragged Trousered Philanthropists*, the fluctuating nature of the wage cycle, with its annual slaughter and periodic cut backs, is seen to be devastating primarily because it deprives the male breadwinner of the means to provide for those within the household. Thus for the men, home and work are intimately related. It is an image of the home that Newman first contemplates when he learns that he has been laid off by Hunter:

> Newman stood in the darkening room feeling as if his heart had turned to lead. There rose before his mind the picture of his home and family. He could see them as they were at this very moment, the wife probably just beginning to prepare the evening meal, and the children setting the cups and saucers and other things on the kitchen table. (Tressell 1993: 162)

The darker aspects of the philanthropists' inability to achieve a family wage are everywhere apparent; from Owen's thoughts of suicide in Chapter Six which revolve around a fear of his inability to take responsibility for his family, to Ruth Easton's seduction within the home by her lodger, Slyme. In effect, Ruth's sexual "fall" is written as a direct consequence of her husband's inability to provide sufficient upkeep for his home and his family (which necessitates the couple's taking in of a lodger in the first place). Easton's complicity in Ruth's seduction is stressed by Owen and his wife's sympathy for the latter, and in Owen's conviction that Easton must accept responsibility for his part in the collapse of the home.

The spatial geography of this model, based upon the breadwinning husband and his dependent wife and children, has been heavily critiqued as relying upon a redundant spatial separation that necessitates a binary understanding of gender and place (note the level of stasis in Newman's domestic fantasy above). It was a way of seeing family life that both the Fabian Women's Group and the Women's Co-operative Guild, the largest working-class women's group of the period, took issue with. Some readers of Tressell have identified a heightened concern in *The Ragged Trousered Philanthropists* with the male world of work (outside), alongside a shorn-up fantasy of the sanctity of the home. Eileen Yeo argues for this way of reading the text:

> We often come home after work with Tressell to find, in the good times anyway, a scrupulously clean and cosy house with a table set invitingly for tea. [...] All of the women in the novel are portrayed as more or less exposed, languishing, collapsed or ill. They all depend on male support or rescue. (Yeo 1988: 84–5)

Yet such a way of reading the working-class woman at home in the text is misleading. Though the women are certainly defined by their relation to the male breadwinner (those in search of anything other than the heterosexual figure of completion in the novel's gender politics will be sorely disappointed), the domestic interior is hardly a place of political retreat. The women within the home are seen to be actively involved in work (paid and unpaid) and the community. Mary Linden is engaged in sweated outwork, Nora Owen works as a charwoman, and Bert White's mother (as a widow) is forced to provide for her family single-handedly. Indeed, whilst the family wage debate raged, it has been questioned to what extent working-class women prior to the First World War could actually partake in bourgeois ideals concerning the gendered separation of interior and exterior spaces. In *Wage-Earning Women and their Dependents*, published on behalf of the Fabian Women's Group, Ellen Smith estimated that the women breadwinners of England and Wales could be supporting up to four million dependents (Smith 1915: 35). The prominence given to Ruth's financial management within the domestic interior (which is not merely self-denying but sufficiently complex as to frustrate and confuse her husband), is also suggestive of a more mutually productive occupation of space than critics would suggest. There is a mass of historical literature on the importance of the mother's financial management in the working-class household of this period, much of it inspired by a revisionist politics that challenges renderings of the working-class woman as passive body within the home (see e.g. Bourke 1994). What is more, the friendships between the philanthropists' wives are one of the most important sites of support for the families (in both emotional and financial terms), and for the possibility of narrative resolution.

REPRODUCING THE HOUSE: LAWRENCE

> On whatever theoretical horizon we examine it, the house would appear to have become the topography of our intimate being
>
> Bachelard 1958: xxxii

Since the publication of *Sons and Lovers*, critics have sought to interpret its protagonist, Paul Morel, as a twentieth-century Oedipus. The fact of Lawrence's mother's death in December 1910, for whom the novel was originally conceived, not to mention the author's fierce disinclination to be associated with the ideas of Freud, has provoked a variety of psychoanalytic readings of the text.[4] Framed in terms of Paul's desire to replace his father within the home, both financially and sexually, "I'm the man in the house now," the textual suggestions for such a reading are manifold (Lawrence 1948: 112). What is most often lacking in such accounts however, is an adequate consideration of the immediate context in which Lawrence was writing and the ways in which a growth of discourse about the self, and in particular the psychoanalytic self (as the ultimate interior) may have impinged upon the ways of seeing the home in the text. Virginia Woolf's oft-quoted comment, "on or about December 1910 human character changed," points to a shift that has become part of a cultural narrative that writes a Victorian discourse of character (moral conduct and public duty) against an evolving concern with the development of personality as interiority. Matthew Thomson elaborates:

> There was a fundamental reconceptualisation of human psychology in the last decades of the nineteenth and the first decades of the twentieth centuries. [...] The role of the mind in mediating between experience and action or knowledge was radically problematised, and in the process the architecture of consciousness was opened up as a territory for exploration. (Thomson 2001: 100)

What is of most significance in locating these burgeoning ways of seeing alongside Lawrence's *Sons and Lovers* is their spatial geography. The psychological landscape that was emerging during these years, with its discovery of new "levels" of the mind (whether subconscious, unconscious, subliminal or superconscious) mapped itself in explicitly spatial terms.

As in *The Ragged Trousered Philanthropists*, imagining the home is crucial to the narrative gaze and action of the text in *Sons and Lovers*. From the opening of the narrative, with the narrator's sweeping survey of Bestwood, the Morels' house is the text's central place of desire. The house which predominates in the novel's opening pages, with its unique positioning as an end terrace enabling Mrs Morel to enjoy "a kind of aristocracy among the other women of the 'between' houses," is inspired by Lawrence's second Eastwood home:

> The Bottoms consisted of six blocks of miners' dwellings, two rows of three, like the dots on a blank-six domino, and twelve houses in a block. This double row of dwellings sat at the foot of the rather sharp slope from Bestwood, and looked out, from the attic windows at least, on the slow climb of the valley towards Selby.
>
> The houses themselves were substantial and very decent. One could walk all round, seeing little front gardens [...] neat front windows, little porches, little privet hedges, and dormer windows for the attics. But that was outside; that was the view on to the uninhabited parlours of all the colliers' wives. The dwelling-room, the kitchen, was at the back of the house, facing inward between the blocks, looking at a scrubby back-garden, and then at the ash-pits. And between the rows, between the long lines of ash-pits, went the alley, where the children played and the women gossiped and the men smoked. [...]
>
> Mrs Morel was not anxious to move into the Bottoms, which was already twelve years old and on the downward path, when she descended to it from Bestwood. But it was the best she could do. (Lawrence 1948: 8–9)

It is here that the Morels' early marital battles are fought, where Morel locks his wife out in the garden in Chapter One and where Mrs. Morel will eventually triumph over her husband to assume moral occupation of the places within it. For the Morel sons, Paul and William, it is the site of the childhood house from which they must strive to individuate. Though the narrative sees Paul occupying a number of different places (Nottingham and Willey Farm being the most important), it is not until the end of the novel and the death of his mother that the childhood home ceases to be the most privileged place in the text for him. His attempts to transfer his affections from Mrs. Morel to first Miriam, and then Clara, are described in terms of the demands of the home:

When he celebrated his twenty-third birthday, the house was in trouble. [...] The house, moreover, needed his support. He was pulled in all directions. (Lawrence 1948: 327–8)

What is significant about Paul's negotiation of the "Mutter-complex," and recalling those discourses elaborated above which sought out the mother as the final resting point for the gaze inside the working-class interior, is the way in which he most closely associates his mother with the home. Seeking to write Mrs. Morel as a known and defined place, Paul thinks of her in terms of the four-square enclosure of the house, "there was one place in the world that stood solid and did not melt into unreality: *the place where his mother was*" (Ibid: 273, my italics). Throughout the novel the reader is encouraged to share in this filial gaze with its stable positioning of the mother within the home. There is something of an erotics of domesticity at play in the way in which Paul watches his mother at work inside the domestic interior:

> So after dinner he lay down on the sofa, [...] once roused, he opened his eyes to see his mother standing on the hearthrug with the hot iron near her cheek. [...] Paul loved the way she crouched and put her head on one side. Her movements were light and quick. It was always a pleasure to watch her. [...] The room was warm and full of the scent of hot linen. (Ibid: 85–6)

With the dissolution of the home after his mother's death, Paul's loss is written as a spatial uprooting; the loss of one's circumscribed place to the sense of a larger, unknown space:

> On and on! And he had no place in it! Whatever spot he stood in, there he stood alone. From his breast, from his mouth, sprang the endless space, and it was there behind him, everywhere. [...] There was no time, only Space. (Ibid: 496, 510)

The pull of the childhood home for Paul and this giving up of a sense of place to the otherness of an exterior space is pre-empted in the text by his brother William's trajectory. There is a very real sense in which William's death is written in terms of his inability to move from the site of the house. Whilst living in London and courting the flighty Miss Western (significantly known as "Gypsy"), William's anxiety of origins is reflected in his loss of place. Returning to his childhood home for a second Christmas (this time with a lady but no presents), his attempt to allow an outside voyeur into the intimacy of the family kitchen leaves them both feeling dislocated:

> She glanced round the kitchen. It was small and curious to her. [...] She felt strange, not able to realize the people, not knowing how to treat them. (Ibid: 145, 147)

As he becomes increasingly unsure of both his sense of class and his sense of self, William starts to anxiously return home, seeking some of that primal certainty which Paul also locates in the mother and the domestic interior, "he went away on Sunday midnight, seeming better *and more solid* for his two days at home" (Ibid: 168, my italics). Yet William is eventually overcome, incapable of managing the possibility for the simultaneity of the childhood home and the city. In *The Poetics of Space*, Bachelard comments that "the space we love is unwilling to remain permanently enclosed" (Bachelard 1958: 53). In William's case, the domestic interior not only fails to remain enclosed, but becomes all-engulfing. The sinister nature of this too-powerfully experienced continuity can be seen in the way in which the domestic chores of the home come to be written upon William's body. Mrs. Morel's earlier token of love for her son, "it was a joy to her to have him proud of his collars. [...] She used to rub away at them with her little convex iron, to polish them, till they shone from the sheer pressure of her arm," ultimately belies an overwhelming presence (Lawrence 1948: 73). The pneumonia which kills William is diagnosed as "starting under the chin where the collar chaffed, and spreading over the face" before it gets to the brain (Ibid: 169). This treatment of the domestic interior as a potentially smothering place of engulfment for the male self is shared in a short story which preceded *Sons and Lovers*, "The Odour of Chrysanthemums" (1911).

Yet however much the reader might be seduced otherwise, neither the house, nor Mrs. Morel within it, attain the kind of solidity of place as a guarantor of meaning that William and Paul seek to invest them with. The childhood home moves three times during the course of the narrative; from the four-square enclosure of "The Bottoms," to the more open expanse of Scargill Street where the house sits on the brow of a hill commanding a view of the "wide, dark valley" below, to a further house nearby after William's death (Ibid: 78). Here Mrs. Morel takes possession of the garden, the immediate outside:

> The garden was an endless joy to her. Paul was thankful for her sake at last to be in a house with a long garden that went down to a field. Every morning after breakfast she went out and was happy pottering about in it. (Ibid: 203)

Indeed, despite Paul and Williams's way of seeing their mother within the home, she is in fact constantly positioned outside its parameters. Whilst in Chapter One, Mrs. Morel feels envious of her husband's ability to indulge in a ten-mile walk to Nottingham, and her enjoyment of "The Wakes" is curtailed through her sense of responsibility to the house, through the course of the text she journeys more than any of the other characters. The distances Morel covers largely revolve around the immediate locality (fields, pubs, the mine), yet Mrs. Morel is seen in Nottingham, London, Lincoln, on vacations at the seaside and at Willey Farm. She also finds a political place outside the home in the Women's Guild:

> It is true, from off the basis at the Guild, *the women could look at* their homes, at the conditions of their own lives, and find fault. (Ibid: 68)

This kind of space is comparable to that enjoyed by the wives of the philanthropists in their network of female friendships in Tressell's novel.

Thus in *The Ragged Trousered Philanthropists* and *Sons and Lovers*, Tressell and Lawrence draw upon a proliferation of contemporary discourses centered upon looking into the houses of the working classes, and a larger literary tradition concerned with navigating the urban landscape and writing the working-classes into fiction. Just as their lived relation as embodied, and classed, individuals influences the way in which they reproduce the home as a site for action and contemplation in the texts, so their use of shifting ideas about the self in the pre-war period varies accordingly. In both texts, it is through recourse to the image of the home and the maternal that the narrator seeks to express their attitude towards, and habitation of, a sense of class. For Lawrence, this looking back at the home would continue throughout his literary career, despite only occasional returns to Eastwood after 1910 (the article "Nottingham and the Mining Country" appeared shortly before his death in 1930). For Tressell meanwhile, who died as a pauper in Liverpool in 1911 (and three years before his novel would finally make it into print) home was not an identifiable source of longing, but a place of flux in a life of poverty and working-class migration.

NOTES

1. *Sons and Lovers* was published on the 29th May 1913 by the London-based Duckworth & Co. The first edition of *The Ragged Trousered Philanthropists* was published by the London house of Grant Richards on 23rd April 1914. This was notoriously edited by Jessie Pope who, at the request of Grant Richards, drastically reduced the length of the novel and tampered with its moral and political message (most notably, she concluded the novel not with Owen's vision of 'the risen sun of Socialism' but with his contemplation of suicide in Chapter 34; Tressell 1993: 587). It is now a commonplace in Tressell criticism to acknowledge the exhaustive work of Fred Ball, who recovered the original manuscript of the text after the Second World War. Ball's work led to the re-publication of the novel in full, as Tressell had originally conceived of it, by the London-based Lawrence & Wishart in 1955.

2. Rowntree's *Study of Town Life*, carried out in York, was published in 1901, whilst the final volume of Booth's *Life and Labour of the People of London* was published in 1902. Concern about the medical unfitness of those who offered themselves up for service in the Boer war campaign led to the establishment of the National Efficiency Movement and an Inter-departmental Committee on Physical Deterioration. The latter reported in 1904, stating that it was in the national interest to devote more attention to the welfare of infants and school children.
3. A Housing of the Working Classes committee was established by Hastings' Trades Council in September 1900; see Hopper (1993).
4. The first psychoanalytic review of the text, written by the American psychologist Alfred Kuttner, was published in *The New Republic* in April 1915.

REFERENCES

Bachelard, Gaston. 1958. *The Poetics of Space*. Translated by Maria Jolas. Boston: Beacon Press; reprinted 1969.

Ballantyne, J. W. 1914. *Expectant Motherhood: Its Supervision and Hygiene*. London: Cassell & Co.

Bloom, Harold. 2000. "Poetic Origins and Final Phases." In David Lodge (ed.) *Modern Criticism and Theory: A Reader*, 2nd edn, pp. 217–229. Harlow: Longman.

Booth, Charles. 1902. *Life and Labour of the People in London*. 17 Vols. London: Macmillan.

Bourke, Joanna. 1994. *Gender, Class and Ethnicity: Working-Class Cultures in Britain 1890–1960*. London: Routledge.

Briggs, Asa. 1983. "'The Language of Class' in Early Nineteenth-Century England." In R. S. Neale (ed.) *History and Class: Essential Readings in Theory and Interpretation*, pp. 2–29. Oxford: Basil Blackwell.

Fitzgerald, Marion. 1915. "How to Visit in the Homes." In *Mothercraft: A Course of Lectures Delivered under the Auspices of The National Association for the Prevention of Infant Mortality*, pp. 33–44. London: The National League for Physical Education and Improvement.

Gilbert, Sandra M., and Susan Gubar. 1979. *The Madwoman in the Attic: The Woman Writer and the Nineteenth Century Literary Imagination*. New Haven: Yale University Press.

Haw, George. 1900. *No Room to Live: The Plaint of Overcrowded London*. London: Wells Gardner Darton & Co.

Haywood, Ian. 1997. *Working-Class Fiction: from Chartism to Trainspotting*. Plymouth: Northcote House Publishers.

Hopper, Trevor. 1993. *Robert Tressell's Hastings: The Background to the Ragged Trousered Philanthropists*, p. 10. Brighton: Hopper Books

Lawrence, D. H. 1981. "The Odour of Chrysanthemums." In *Short Stories*, edited by Stephen Gill, pp. 44–67. London: J.M Dent & Sons.

——. 1948. *Sons and Lovers*. London: Penguin Books.

Llewelyn Davies, Margaret (ed.) 1915. *Maternity: Letters from Working Women*. London: G. Bell & Sons; reprinted by Virago (1978).

Pember Reeves, Maud, (ed.). 1913. *Round about a Pound a Week*. London: G. Bell & Sons; reprinted by Virago (1979).

Rowntree, B. Seebohm. 1901. *Poverty: A Study of Town Life*. London: Macmillan.

Saleeby, C. W. 1915. "The Problems of the Future." In *Mothercraft: A Course of Lectures Delivered under the Auspices of The National Association for the Prevention of Infant Mortality*, pp. 1–10. London: The National League for Physical Education and Improvement.

Smith, Ellen. 1915. *Wage-Earning Women and their Dependents*. London: The Fabian Society.

Thomson, Matthew. 2001. "Psychology and the 'Consciousness of Modernity' in Early Twentieth-Century Britain." In Martin Daunton and Bernhard Rieger (eds) *Meanings of Modernity; Britain from the Late-Victorian Era to World War II*, pp. 97–118. Oxford: Berg.

Tressell, Robert. 1993. *The Ragged Trousered Philanthropists*. London: Flamingo.

Yeo, Eileen. 1988. "Women and Socialism in Tressell's World." In David Alfred (ed.) *The Robert Tressell Lectures 1981–88*, pp. 79–92. Rochester: Workers Educational Association.

HOME CULTURES

NOTES TO CONTRIBUTORS

- Articles should be approximately 5,000 to 8,000 words (but not exceeding 8,000 words in length unless by prior agreement please).
- They must include a three-sentence biography of the author(s) and an abstract.
- Interviews should not exceed 15 pages and do not require an author biography.
- Exhibition and book reviews are normally 500 to 1,000 words in length but review articles can be between 1,000 and 2,000 words.
- The Publishers will require a disk as well as a hard copy of any contributions.

From time to time, *Home Cultures* plans to produce special issues devoted to a single topic with a guest editor. Persons wishing to organize a topical issue are invited to submit a proposal which contains a 100-word description of the topic together with a list of potential contributors and paper subjects. Proposals are accepted only after a review by the Journal editors and in-house editorial staff at Berg Publishers.

MANUSCRIPTS

- Manuscripts should be submitted to:
  Clare Melhuish, Editorial Administrator, *Home Cultures*, Department of Anthropology, University College London, Gower Street, London WC1E 6BT or to <homecultures@ucl.ac.uk>.
- Manuscripts will be acknowledged and entered into the review process discussed below.
- Manuscripts without illustrations will not be returned unless the author provides a self-addressed stamped envelope.
- Submission of a manuscript to the journal will be taken to imply that it is not being considered elsewhere, in the same form, in any language, without the consent of the editor and publisher. It is a condition of acceptance by the editor of a manuscript for publication that the publishers automatically acquire the copyright of the published article throughout the world. *Home Cultures* does not pay authors for their manuscripts nor does it provide retyping, drawing, or mounting of illustrations.

STYLE

- US spelling and mechanicals are to be used. Authors are advised to consult The Chicago Manual of Style (14th Edition) as a guideline for style. Webster's Dictionary is our arbiter of spelling. We encourage the use of major subheadings and, where appropriate, second-level subheadings.
- Manuscripts submitted for consideration as an article must contain:
  – a title page with the full title of the article, the author(s) name and address
  – a three-sentence biography for each author.
- Do not place the author's name on any other page of the manuscript.

MANUSCRIPT PREPARATION

- Manuscripts must be typed double-spaced (including quotations, notes and references cited), on one side only, with at least one-inch margins on standard paper using a typeface no smaller than 12pts.
- The original manuscript and a copy of the text on disk (please ensure it is clearly marked with the word-processing program that has been used) must be submitted, along with original photographs (to be returned).
- Authors should retain a copy for their records.
- Any necessary artwork must be submitted with the manuscript.

FOOTNOTES

- Footnotes appear as 'Notes' at the end of articles.
- Authors are advised to include footnote material in the text whenever possible.
- Notes are to be numbered consecutively throughout the paper and are to be typed double-spaced at the end of the text
- **(Please do not use any footnoting or end-noting programs which your software may offer as this text becomes irretrievably lost at the typesetting stage.)**

REFERENCES

- The list of references should be limited to, and inclusive of, those publications actually cited in the text.
- References are to be cited in the body of the text in parentheses with author's last name, the year of original publication, and page number—e.g. (Rouch 1958: 45).
- Titles and publication information appear as 'References' at the end of the article and should be listed alphabetically by author and chronologically for each author.
- Names of journals and publications should appear in full. Film and video information appear as 'Filmography'.
- References cited should be typed double-spaced on a separate page.
- References not presented in the style required will be returned to the author for revision.

TABLES

- All tabular material should be part of a separately numbered series of 'Tables'.
- Each table must be typed on a separate sheet and identified by a short descriptive title.
- Footnotes for tables appear at the bottom of the table.
- Marginal notations on manuscripts should indicate approximately where tables are to appear.

FIGURES

All illustrative material: drawings, maps, diagrams, and photographs should be designated 'Figures'. They must be submitted in a form suitable for publication without redrawing.

- Drawings should be carefully done with India ink on either hard, white, smooth-surfaced board or good quality tracing paper. Ordinarily, computer-generated drawings are not of publishable quality.
- Color photographs are encouraged by the publishers.
- Photographs should be glossy prints and should be numbered on the back to key with captions. Whenever possible, photographs should be 8 × 10 inches.
- The publishers also encourage artwork to be submitted as scanned files (300dpi or above ONLY) on disc or via email.
- All figures should be numbered consecutively.
- All captions should be typed double-spaced on a separate page.
- Marginal notations on manuscripts should indicate approximately where figures are to appear.
- While the editors and publishers will use all reasonable care in protecting all figures submitted, they cannot assume responsibility for their loss or damage. Authors are discouraged from submitting rare or non-replaceable materials. It is the author's responsibility to secure written copyright clearance on all photographs and drawings that are not in the public domain.

CRITERIA FOR EVALUATION

Home Cultures is a refereed journal. Manuscripts will be accepted only after review by both the editors and anonymous reviewers deemed competent to make professional judgments concerning the quality of the manuscript.

REPRINTS FOR AUTHORS

Twenty-five reprints of author's articles will be provided to the author free of charge. Additional reprints may be purchased upon request.

A heightened interest in the role of the senses in society is sweeping the social sciences, supplanting older paradigms and challenging conventional theories of representation. Shaped by culture, gender and class, the senses mediate between mind and body, idea and object, self and environment.

This pioneering journal provides a crucial forum for the exploration of this vital new area of inquiry. It brings together groundbreaking work in the social sciences and incorporates cutting-edge developments in art, design and architecture. Every volume contains something for and about each of the senses, both singly and in all sorts of novel configurations.

Prospective readership
+ Sociology & Anthropology
+ Cultural & Media Studies
+ History
+ Visual & Non Visual Arts
+ Psychology

+ **Multi-disciplinary**
+ **Multi-sensory**
+ **International coverage**
+ **Special issues on ground breaking topics**
+ **Book, exhibition and sensory design reviews**

Print: ISSN 1745-8927
Online: ISSN 1745-8935

BERG

New in 2006! | **Special introductory subscription offers!**

The Senses & Society

Edited by:
Michael Bull, University of Sussex
Paul Gilroy, London School of Economics
David Howes, Concordia University
Douglas Kahn, University of California, Davis

Published 3 times a year from 2006 March, July, November

Get 20% off when you subscribe for 2 years!

	Individuals	Institutions
1 year subscription	$70	$289
	£40	£155
2 year subscription	$112 save $28	$462 save $116
	£64 save £16	£248 save £62

All institutional subscriptions include free online access

1 year online only subscription $235   £125 +vat
Please quote order code SS05.

Please call +44 (0) 1767 604 951 to place your order or order online at www.bergpublishers.com

BERG

Drinking Cultures

This timely book looks at alcohol consumption across cultures and what drinking means to the people who consume or, equally tellingly, refuse to consume.

May 2005
PB 1 85973 873 7   £18.99 / $32.95
HB 1 85973 868 0   £55.00 / $99.95

The Taste Culture Reader: Experiencing Food and Drink
Edited by Carol Korsmeyer

Charged with memory, emotion, desire and aversion, taste is arguably the most evocative of the senses. *The Taste Culture Reader* explores the sensuous dimensions of eating and drinking.

August 2005
PB 1 84520 061 6   £19.99 / $34.95
HB 1 84520 060 8   £55.00 / $99.95

Free p&p from www.bergpublishers.com
Also available at all good bookshops or by phoning our order hotlines:
UK +44 (0)1202 665432, USA (888) 330-8477

TEXTILE

The Journal of Cloth & Culture

Edited by Pennina Barnett and Doran Ross

This exciting journal brings together research in an innovative and distinctive academic forum, and will be of interest to all those who share a multifaceted view of textiles within an expanded field. Representing a dynamic and wide-ranging set of critical practices, it provides a platform for points of departure between art and craft; gender and identity; cloth, body and architecture; labour and technology; techno-design and practice - all situated within the broader contexts of material and visual culture.

- **Free online access for print subscribers**
- **International coverage**
- **Heavily illustrated**
- **Annual special issues**
- **Exhibition and book reviews**

'*Accessible, with diverse contributions presented in a readable format...Textile shows that wider cultural interest in 'the crafts' comes when we dare to move beyond the narrow concerns of tradition and technique.*'
Crafts

Published from 2003 March, July, November

20% discount for new subscribers

ISSN 1475-9756

	Individuals		Institutions	
1-year subscription	~~£45~~	**£36**	~~£115~~	**£92**
	~~$78~~	**$62**	~~$205~~	**$164**
2-year subscription	~~£72~~	**£58**	~~£184~~	**£147**
	~~$125~~	**$100**	~~$328~~	**$262**

Please call +44 (0) 1767 604951 to place your order
or order online at www.bergpublishers.com

Please quote order code TTS5.

BERG

Slow Living

'Highly original, exciting and timely, 'Slow Living' brings to the fore current academic and popular debates about postmaterialism and new traditionalism -- there is certainly no other book like it.'
David Bell, MMU

February 2006

PB 1 84520 160 4 £16.99 $29.95
HB 1 84520 159 0 £55.00 $99.95

Wendy Parkins and Geoffrey Craig

FREE P & P FROM WWW.BERGPUBLISHERS.COM
ALSO AVAILABLE AT ALL GOOD BOOKSHOPS OR BY PHONING OUR ORDER HOTLINES:
UK +44 (0)1202 665432 / USA (888) 330-8477

BERG [BÜRG, 1983] N. A CREATIVE PUBLISHER; V.T. TO WORK WITH (Q.V., AUTHORS); ADJ. INDEPENDENT